"That love is inexhaustible, you will be there" forever

THIS BOOK Belongs to

Visit Our Author Page At

amazon.com

Scan me

BICYCLE COLORING BOOK

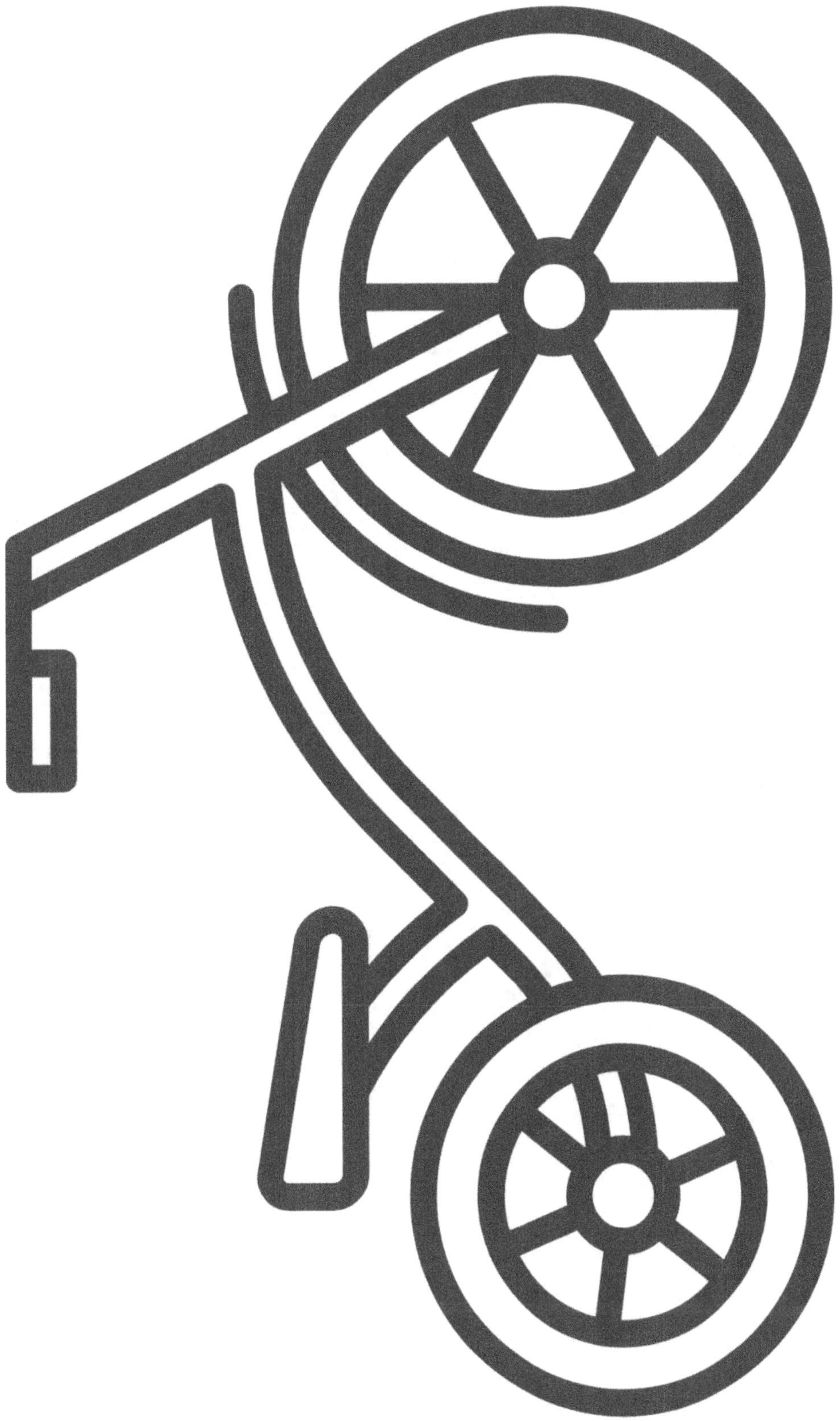

BICYCLE COLORING BOOK

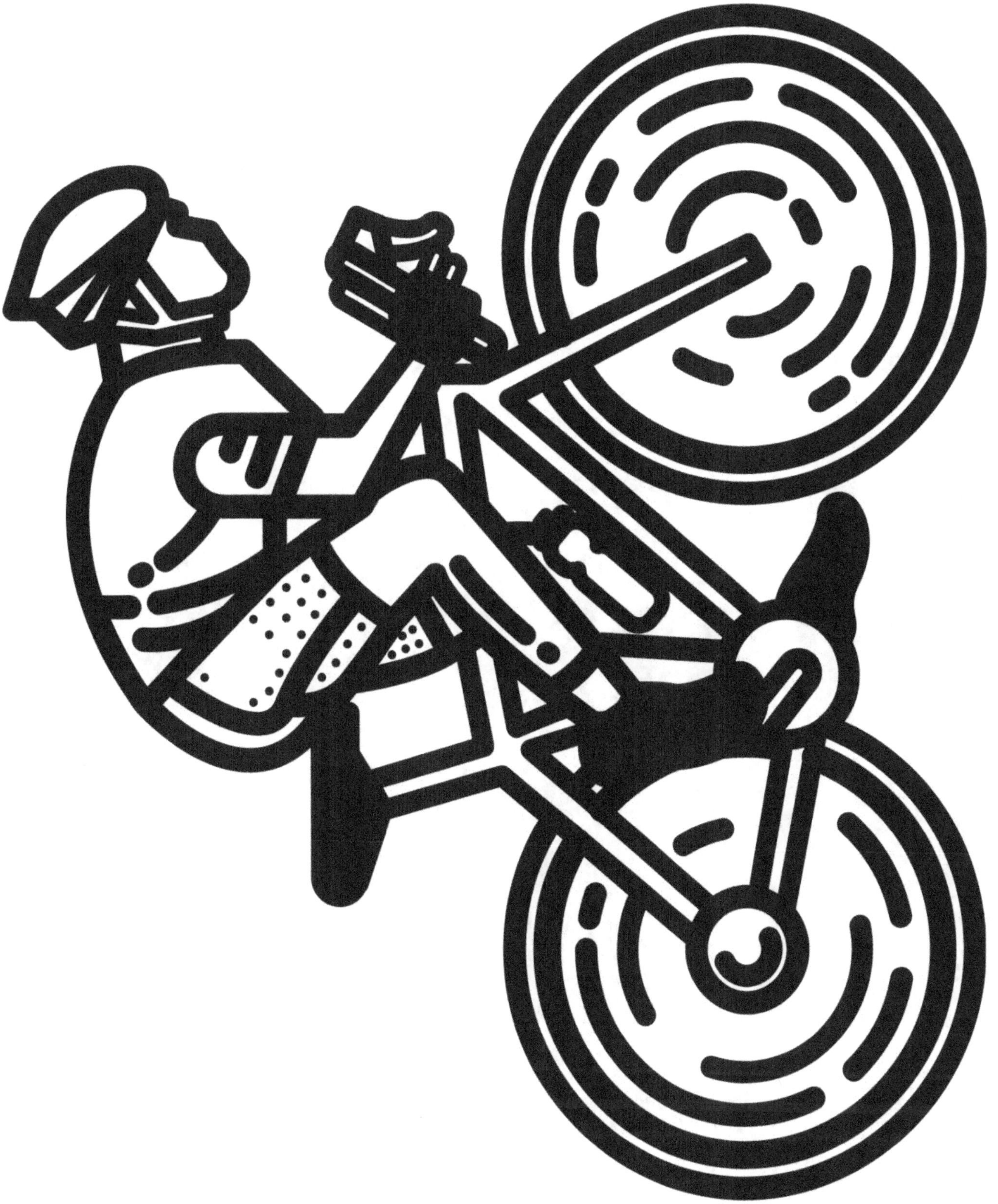

BICYCLE COLORING BOOK

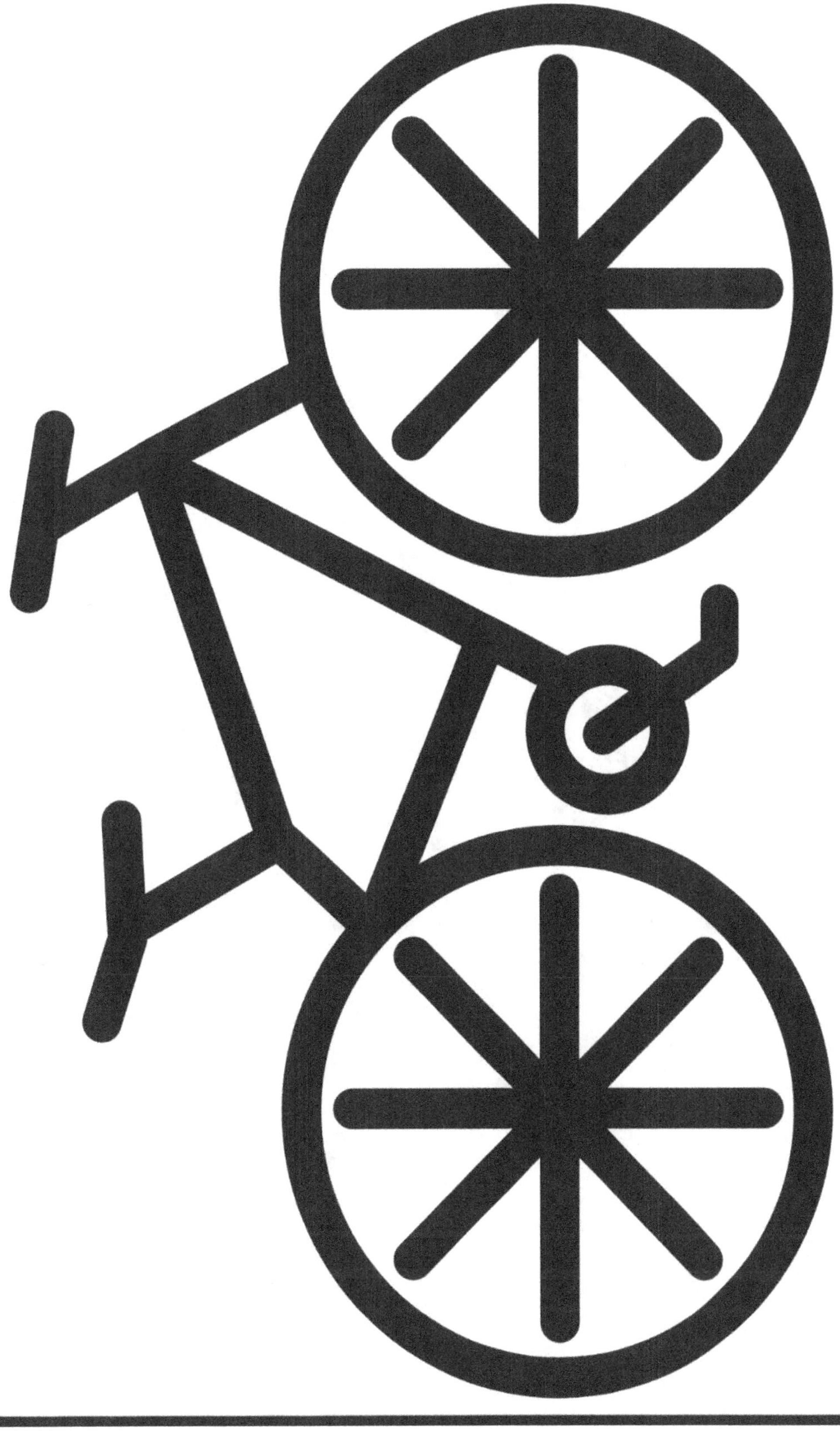

BICYCLE COLORING BOOK

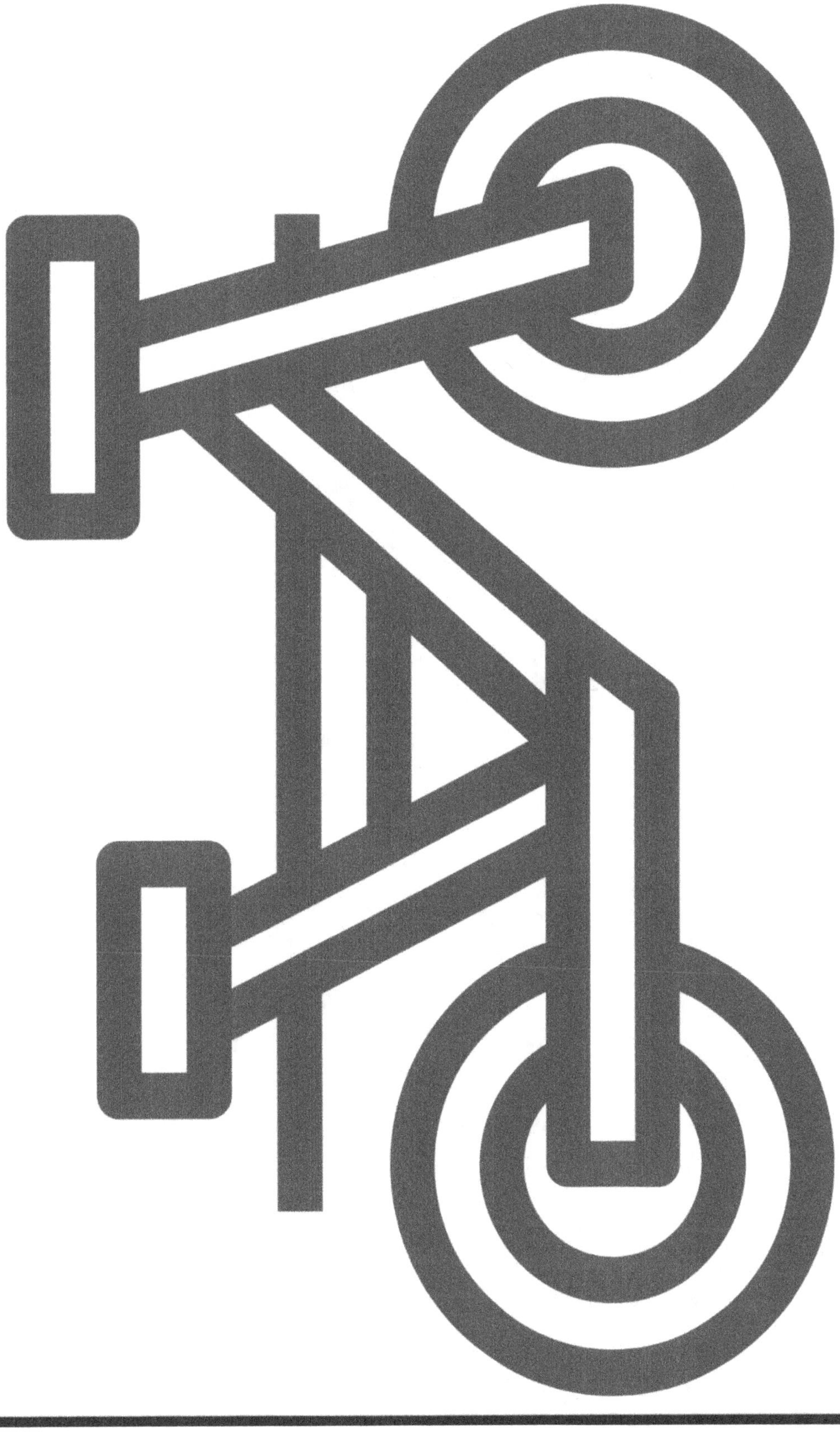

BICYCLE COLORING BOOK

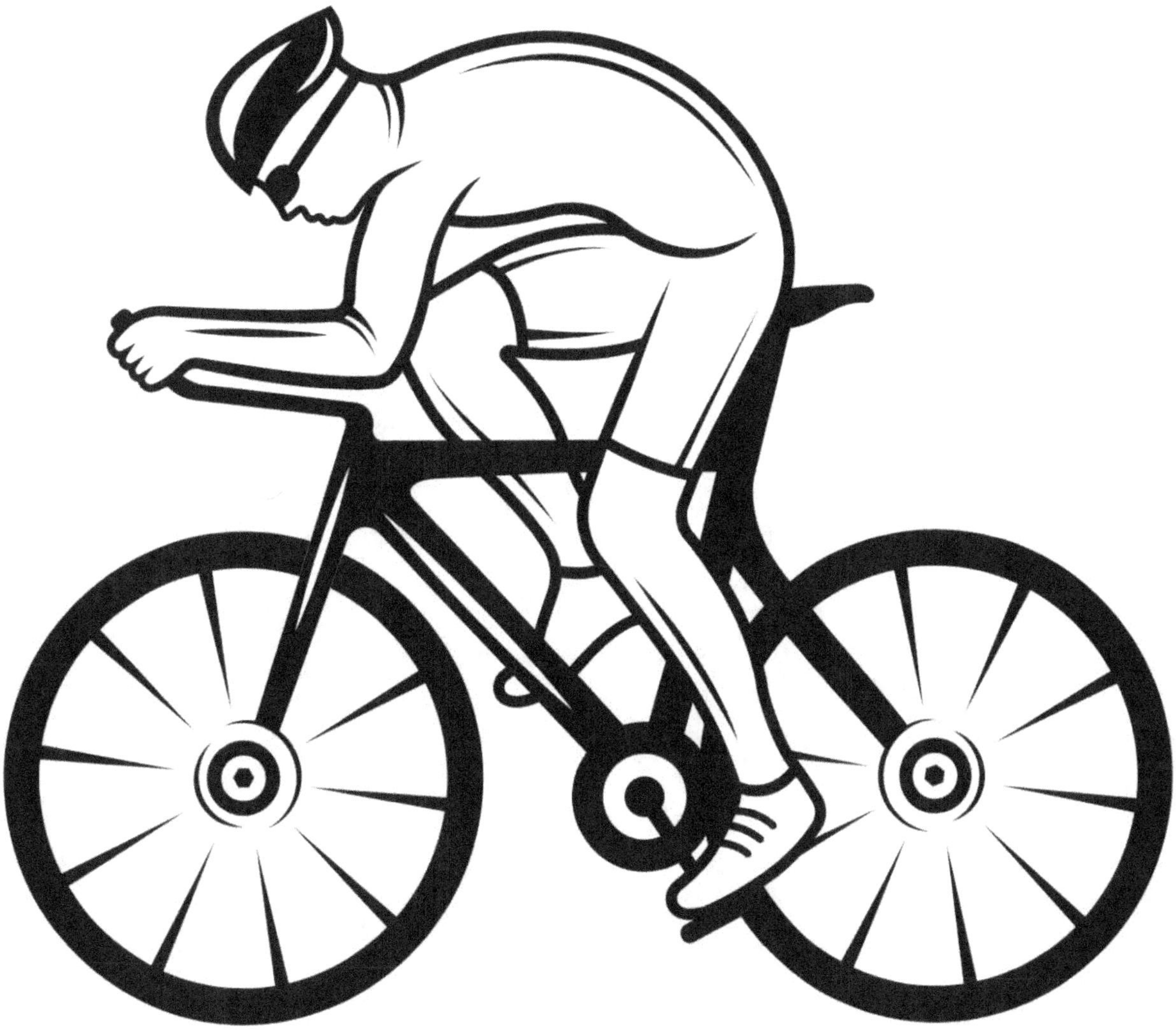

BICYCLE COLORING BOOK

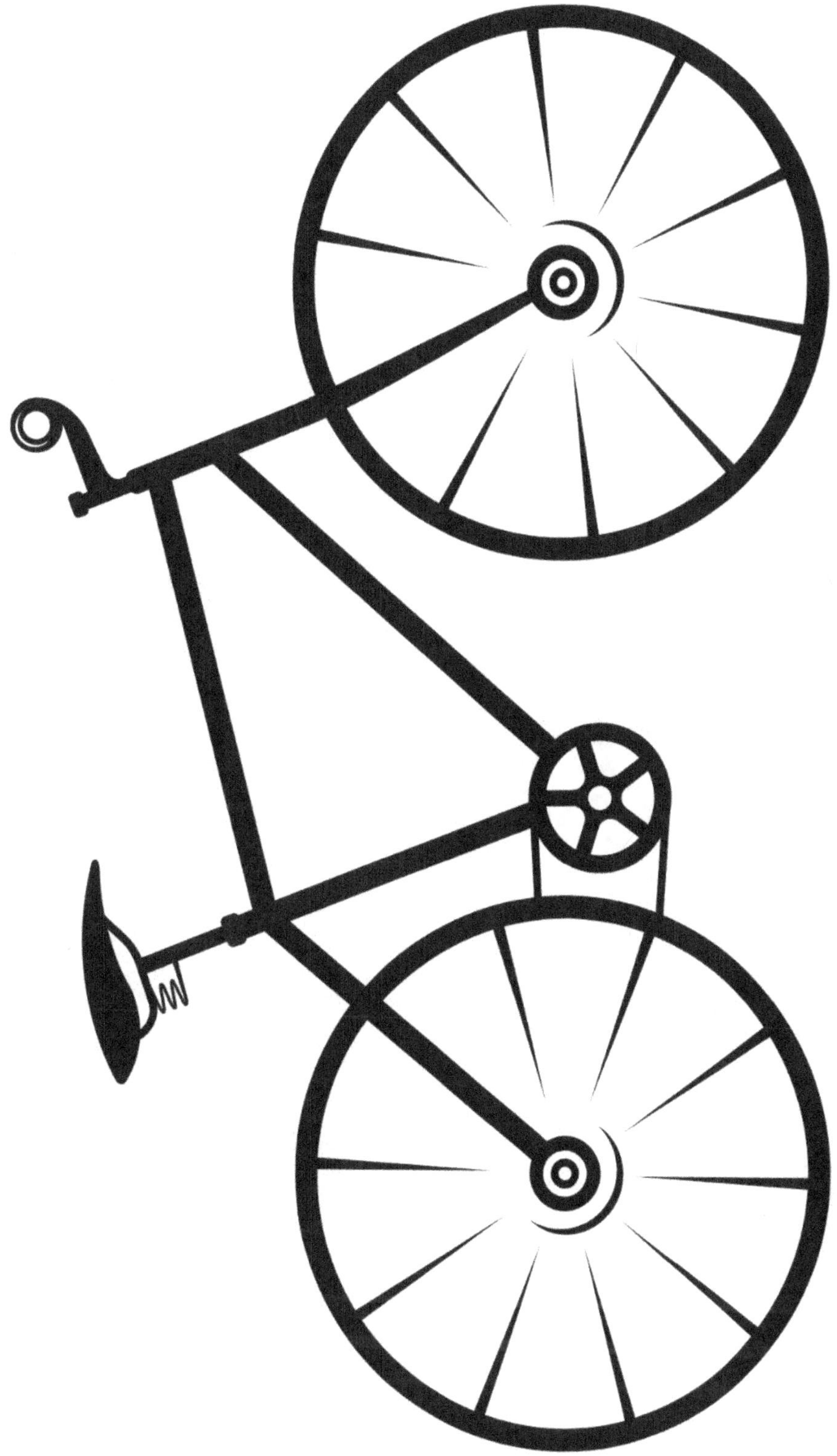

BICYCLE COLORING BOOK

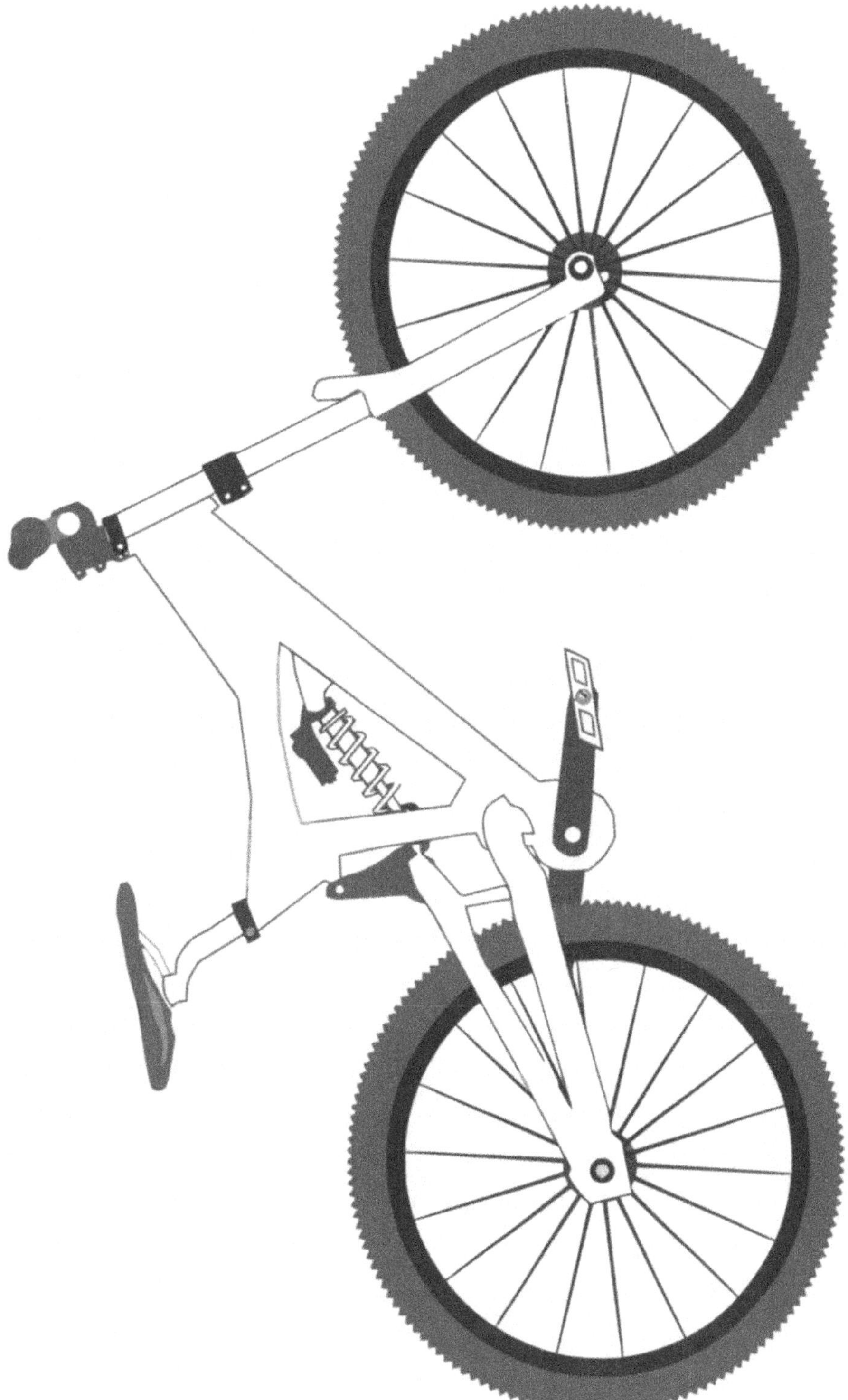

BICYCLE COLORING BOOK

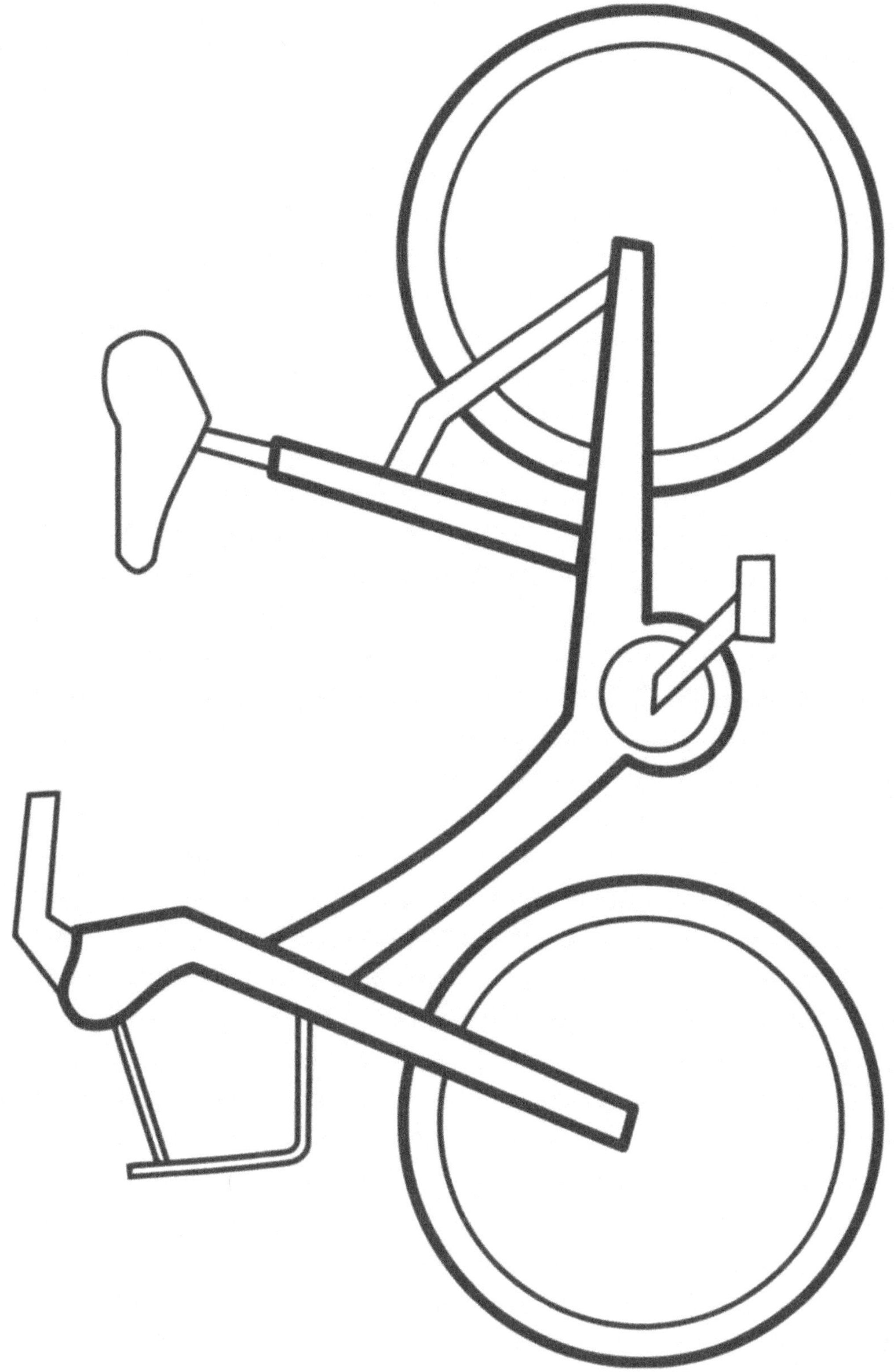

BICYCLE COLORING BOOK

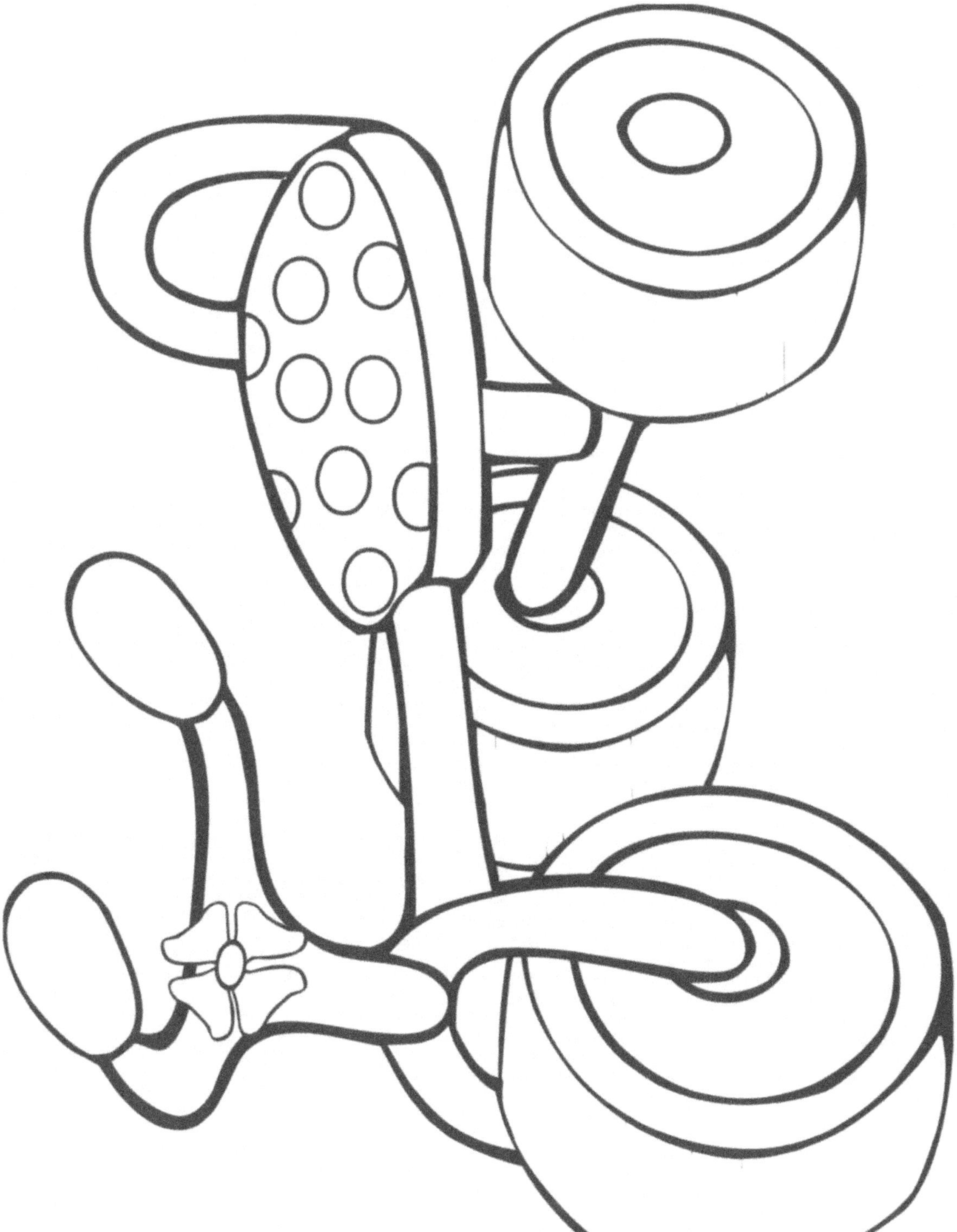

BICYCLE COLORING BOOK

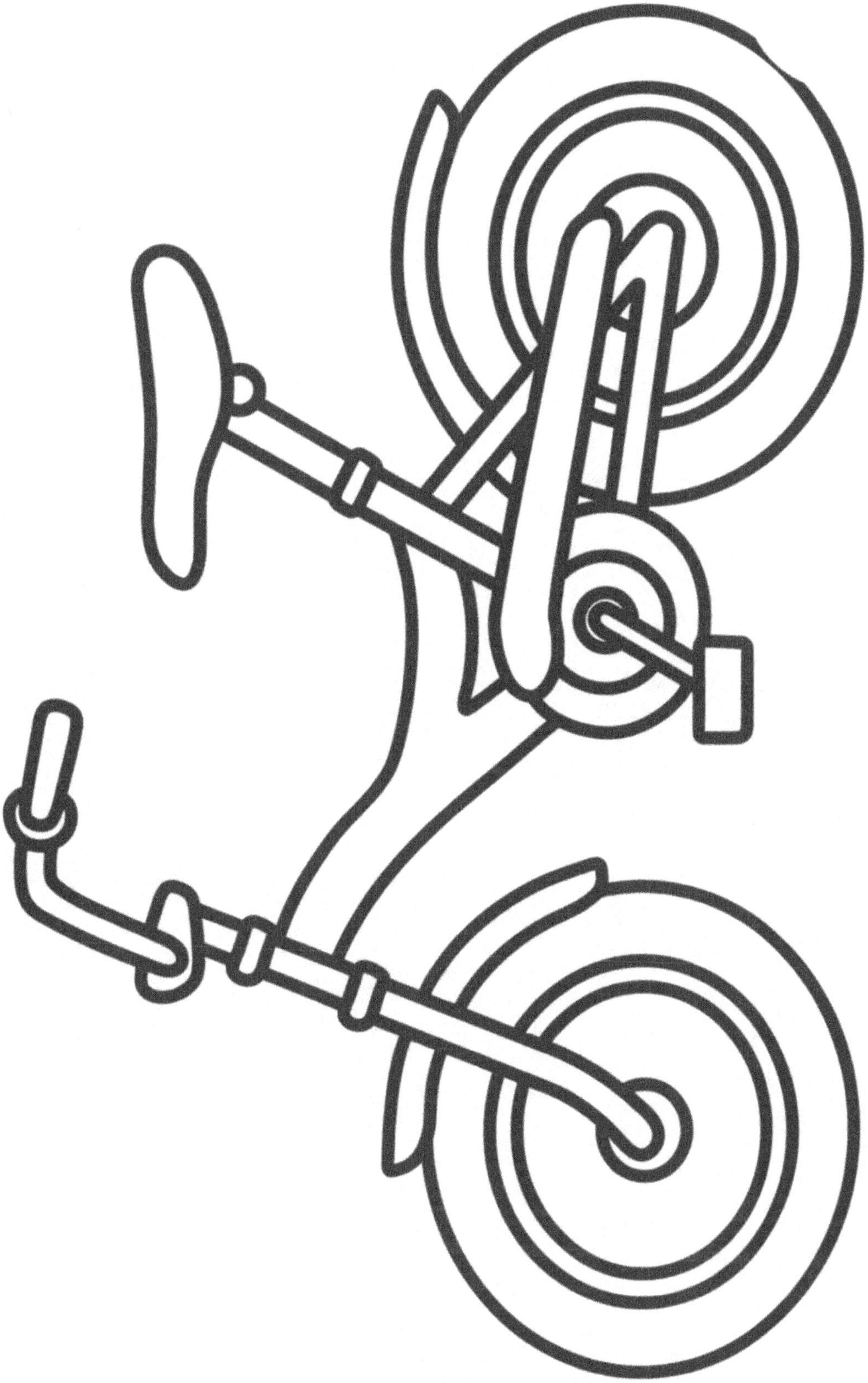

BICYCLE COLORING BOOK

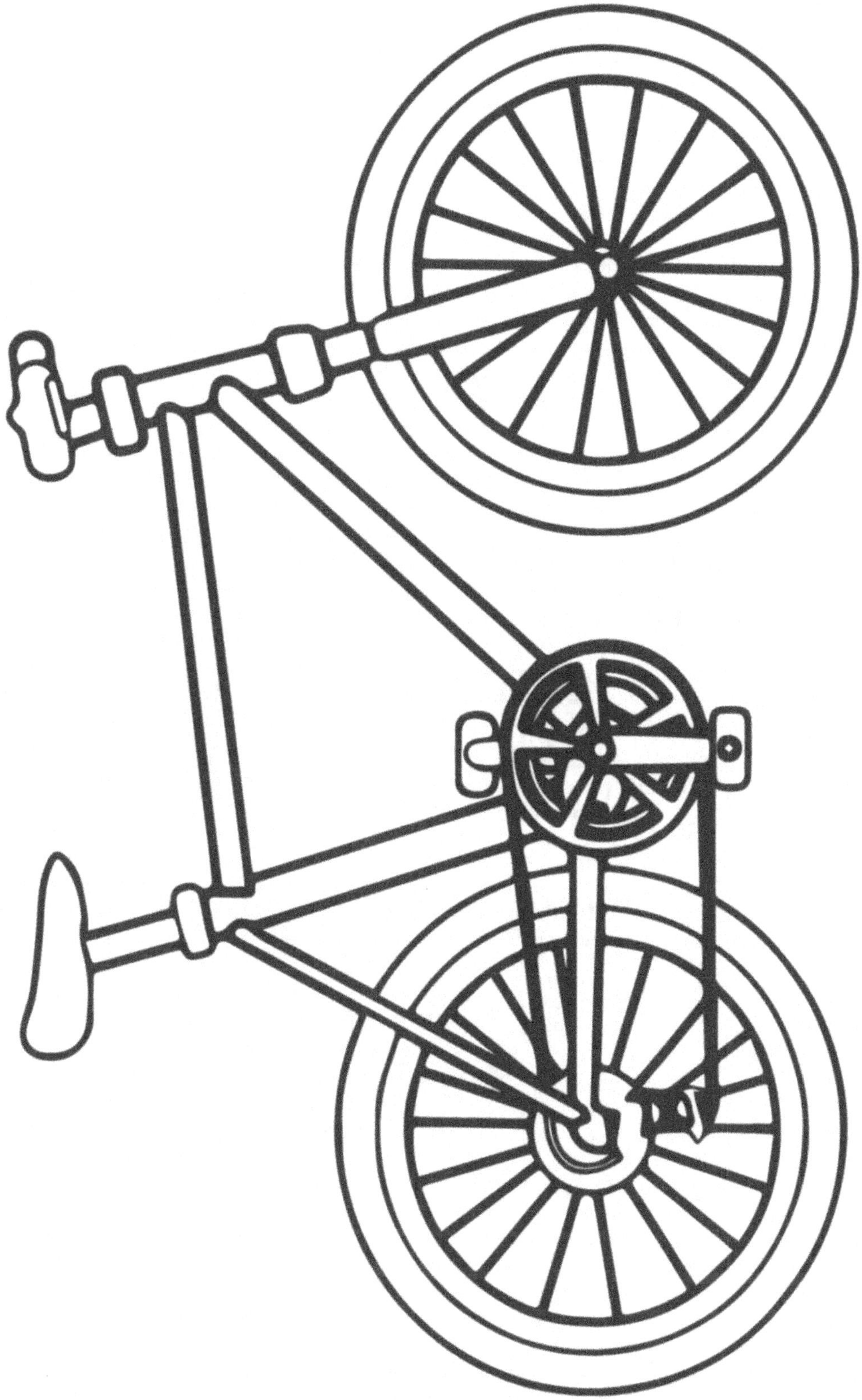

BICYCLE COLORING BOOK

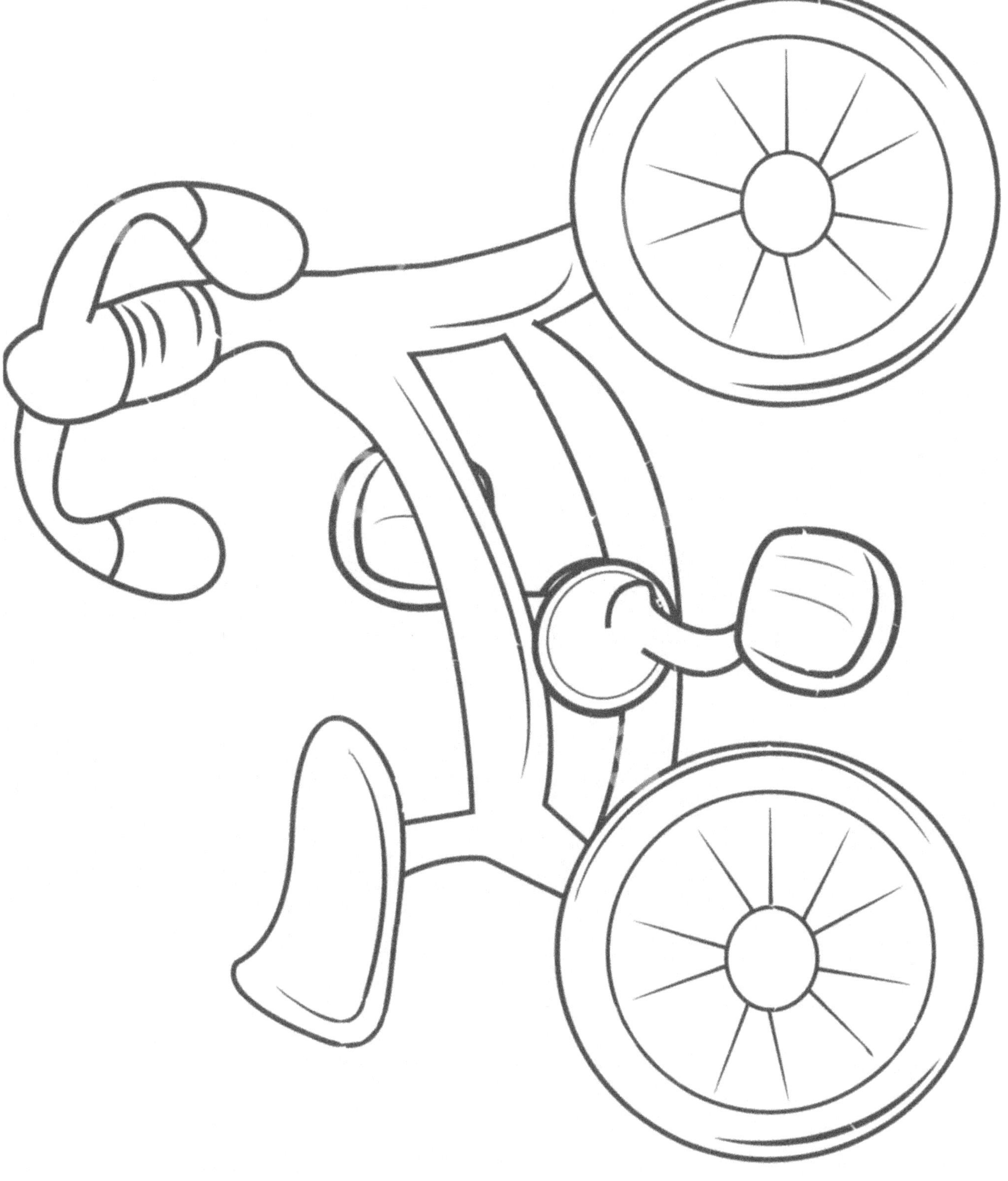

BICYCLE COLORING BOOK

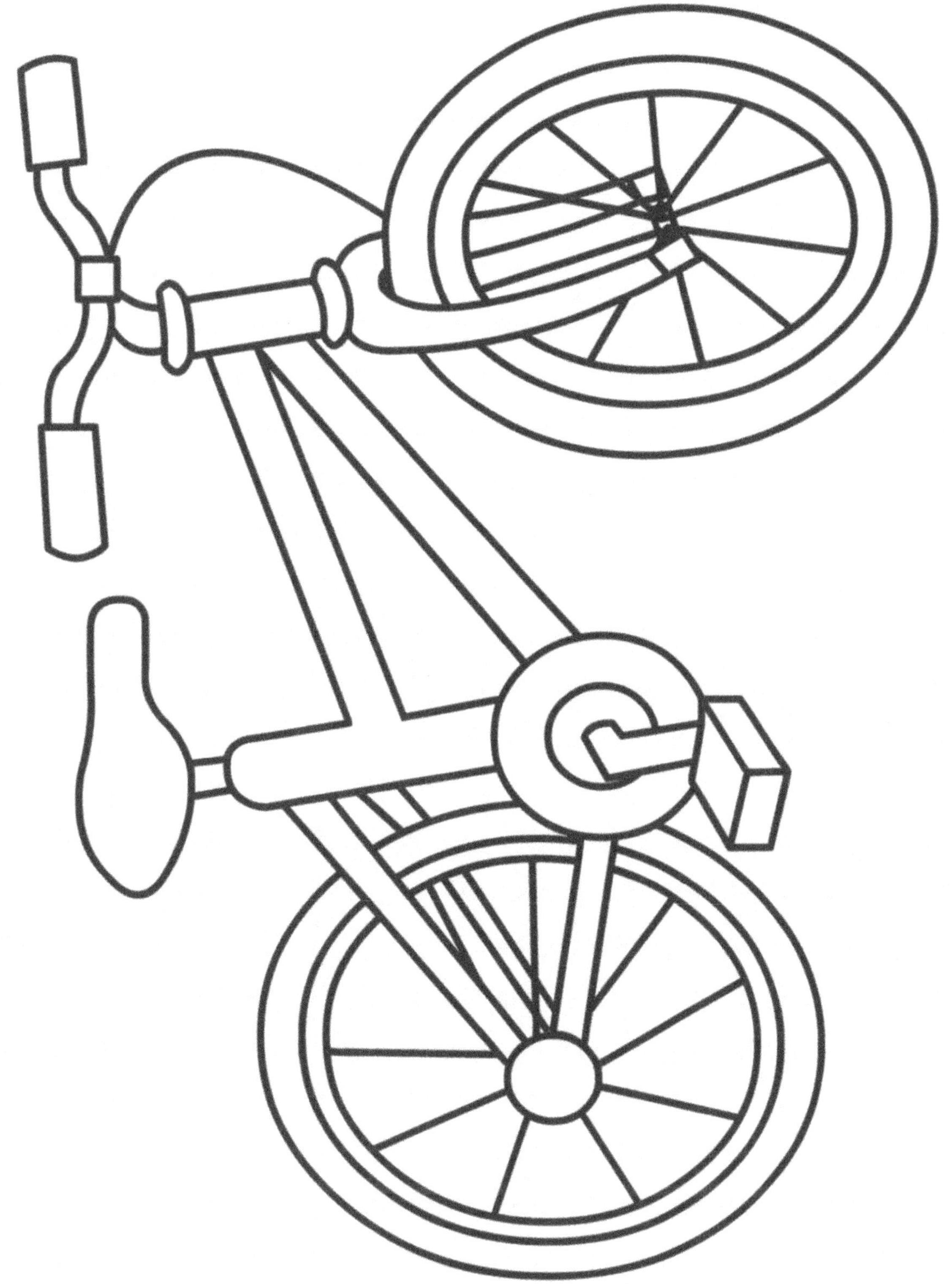

BICYCLE COLORING BOOK

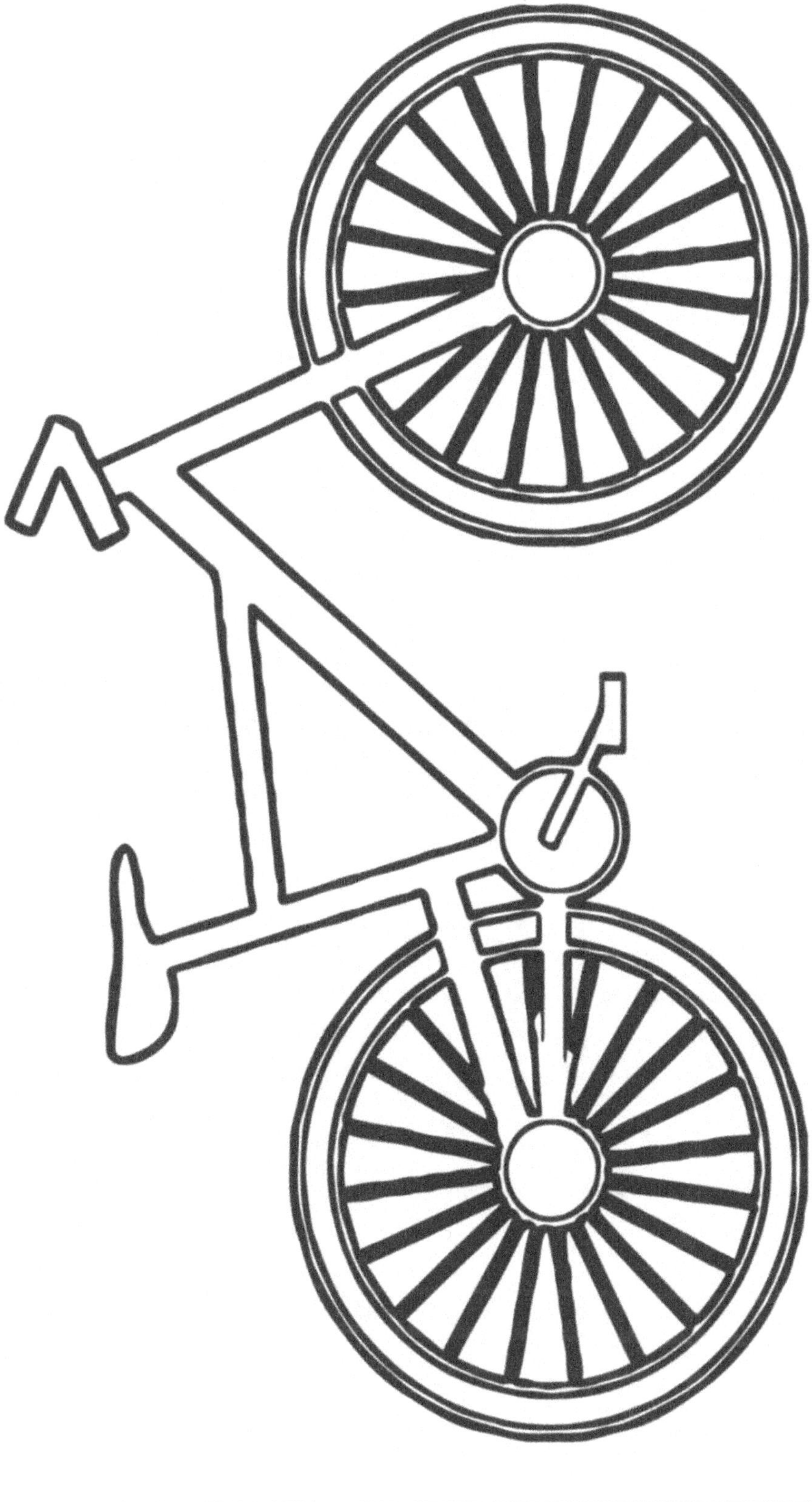

BICYCLE COLORING BOOK

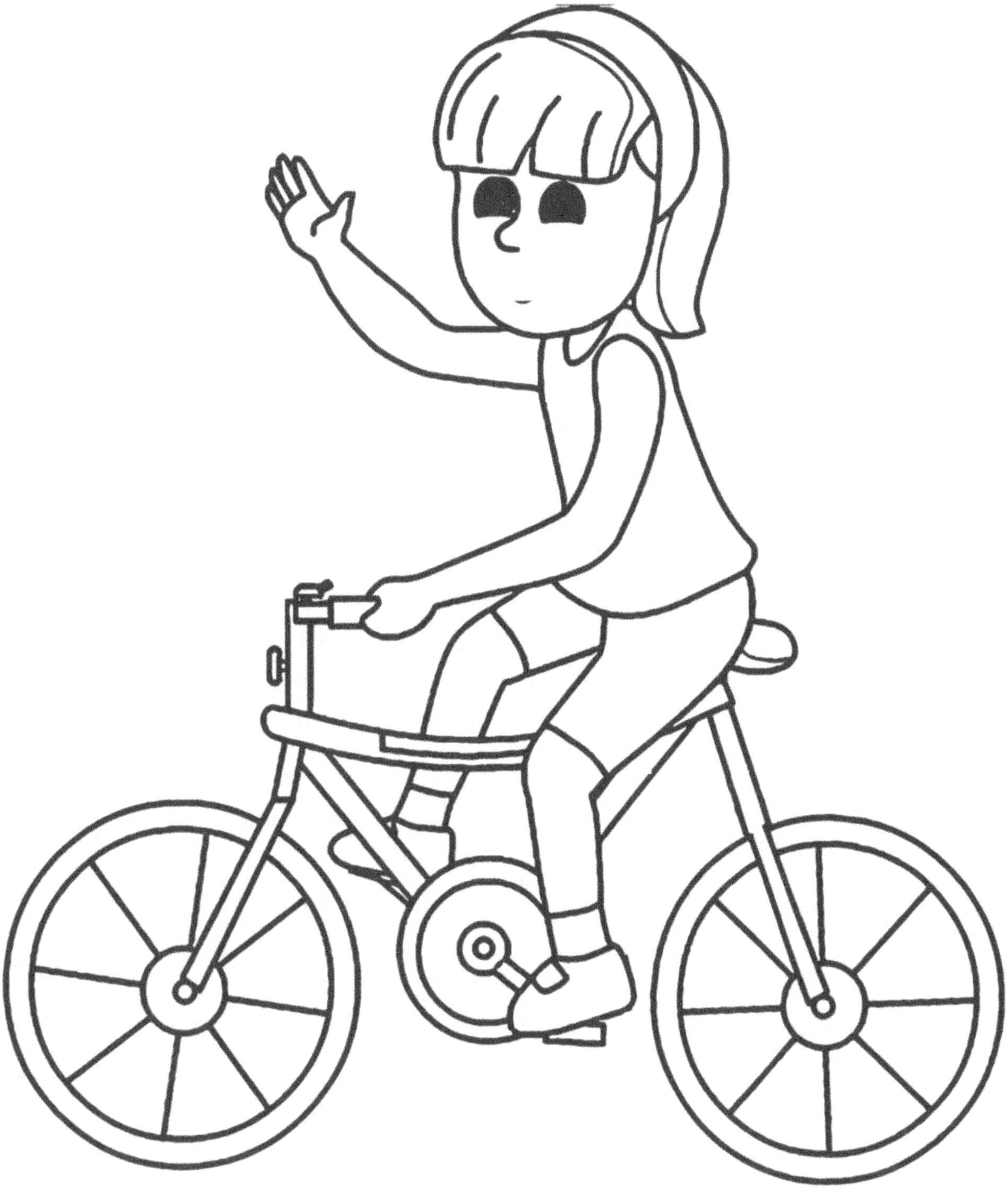

BICYCLE COLORING BOOK

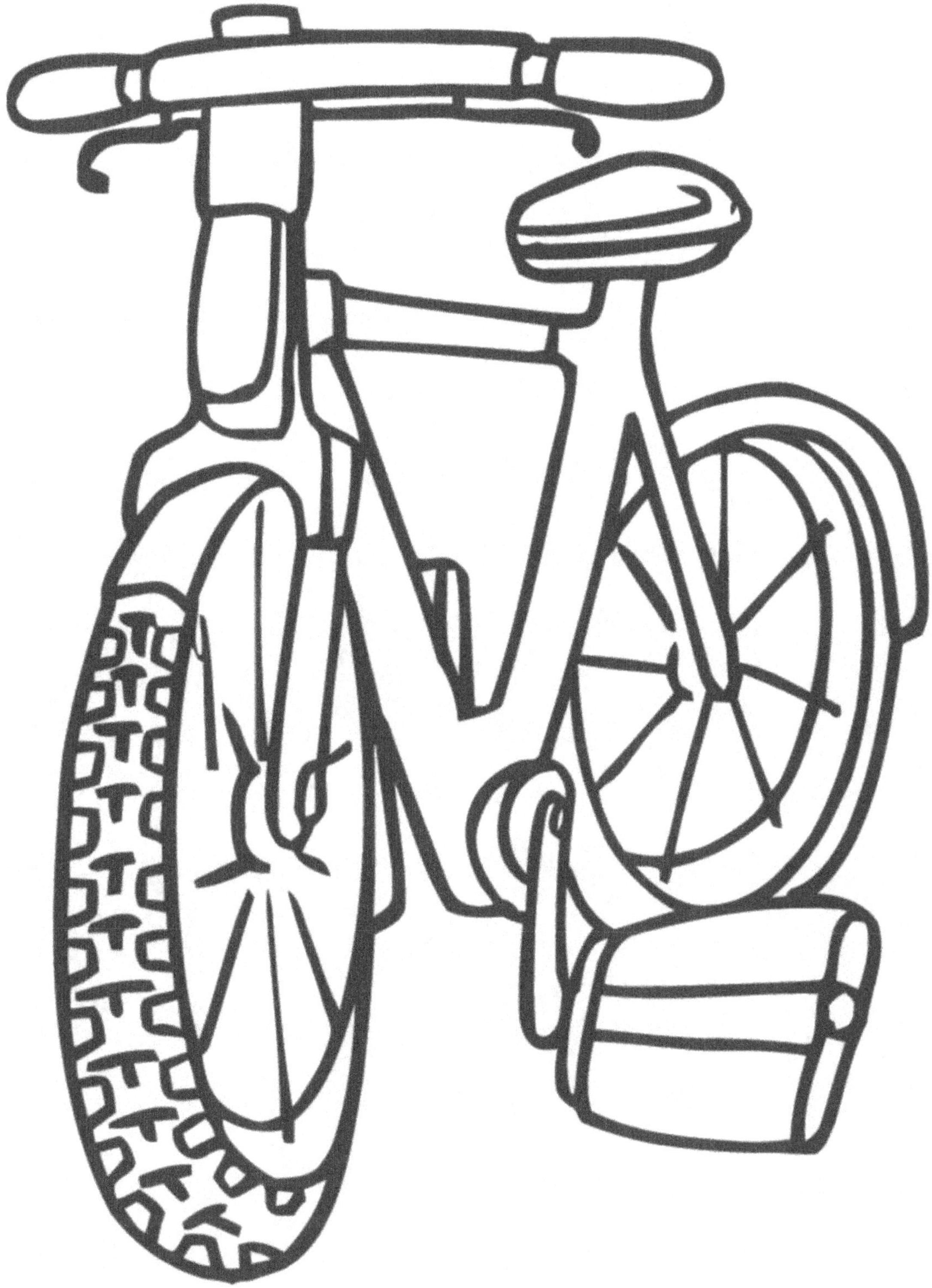

BICYCLE COLORING BOOK

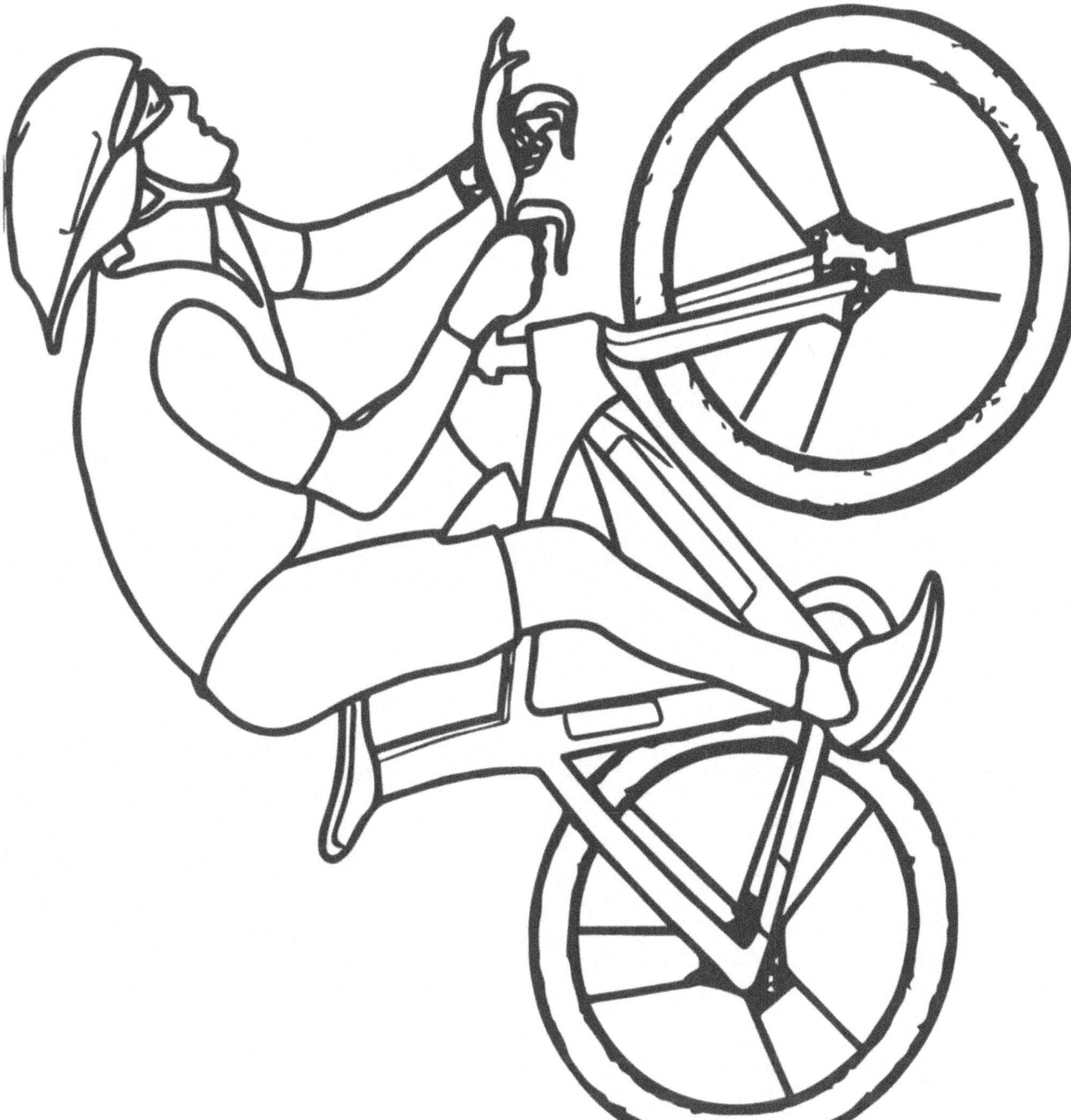

BICYCLE COLORING BOOK

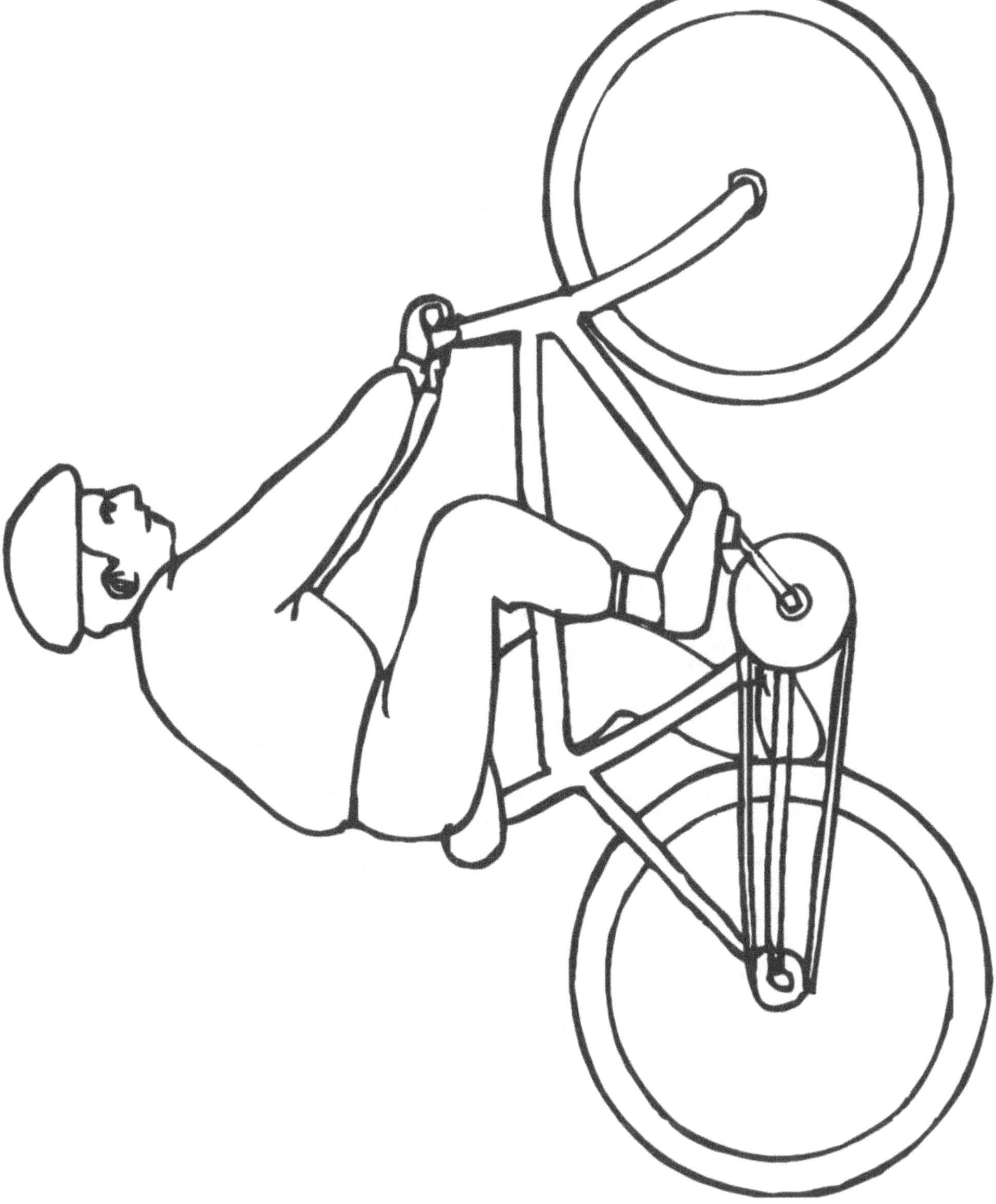

BICYCLE COLORING BOOK

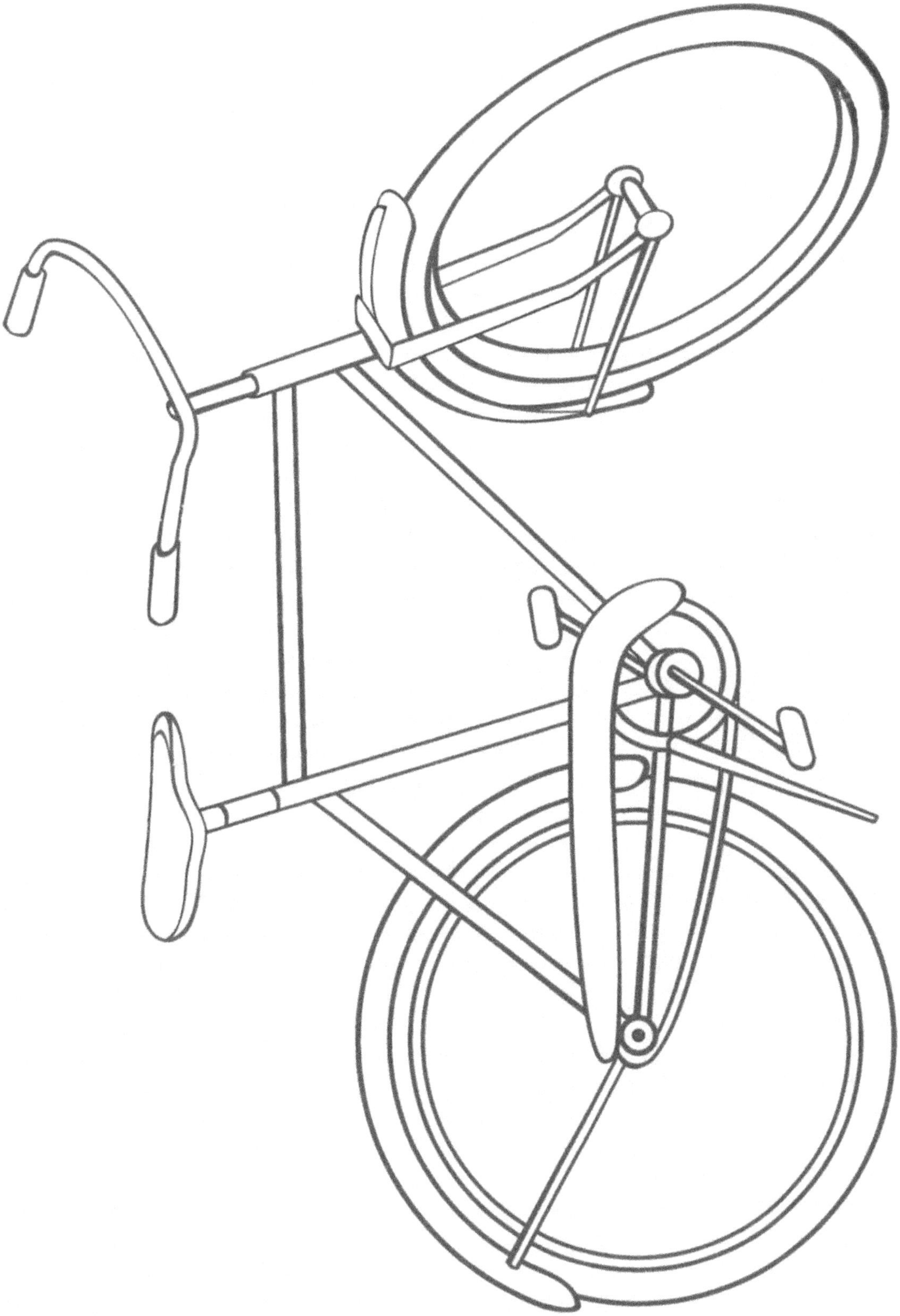

BICYCLE COLORING BOOK

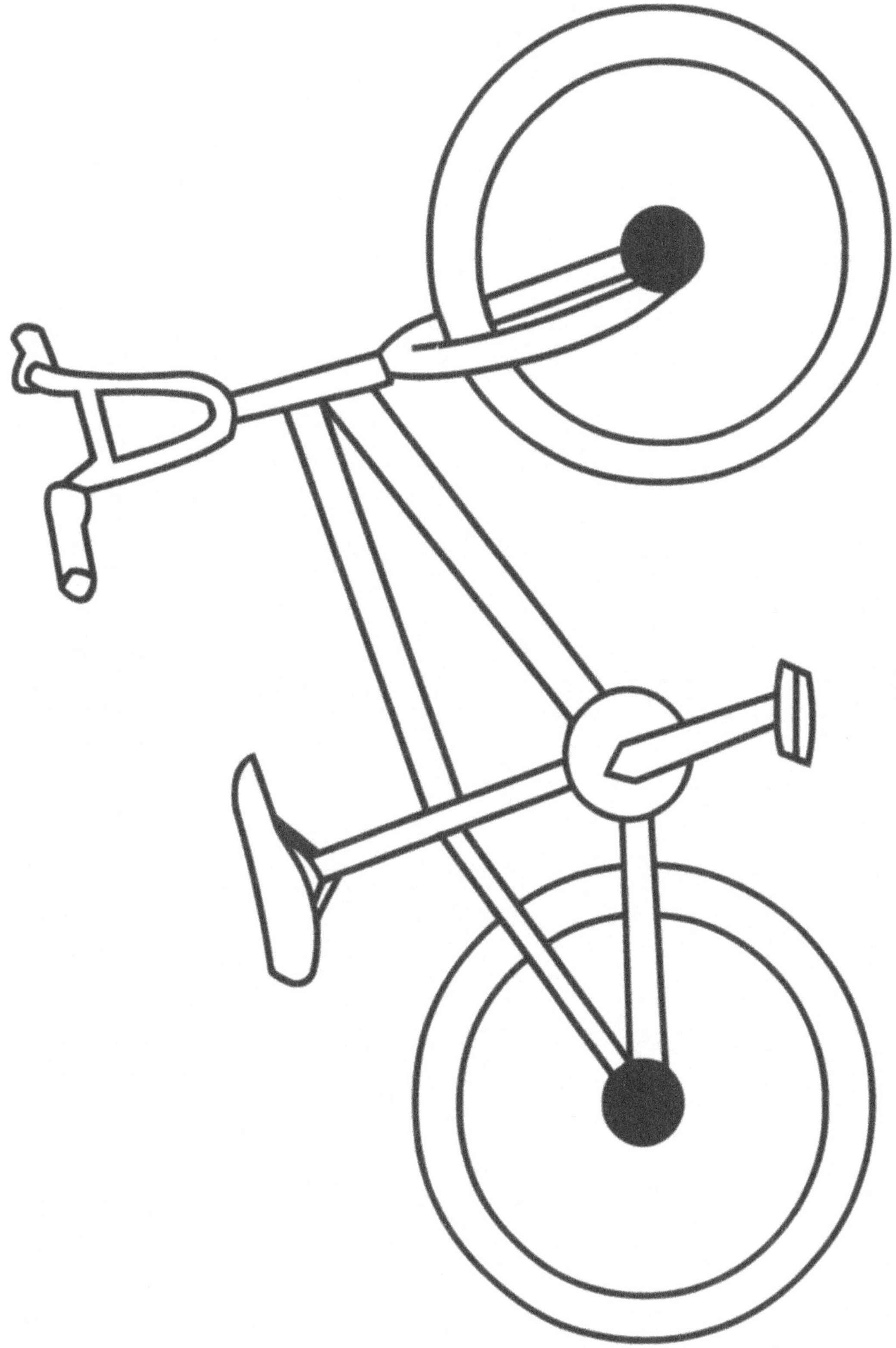

BICYCLE COLORING BOOK

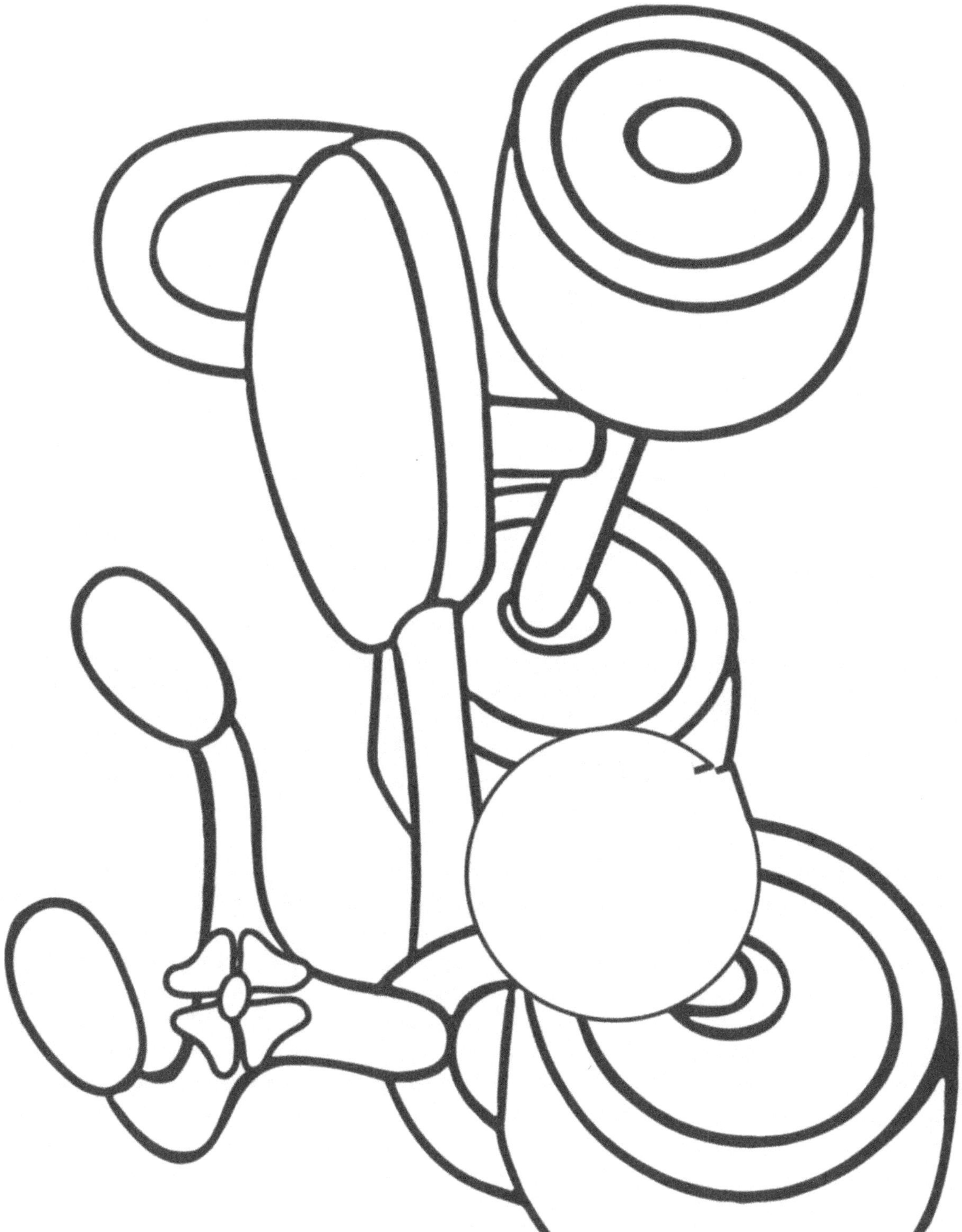

BICYCLE COLORING BOOK

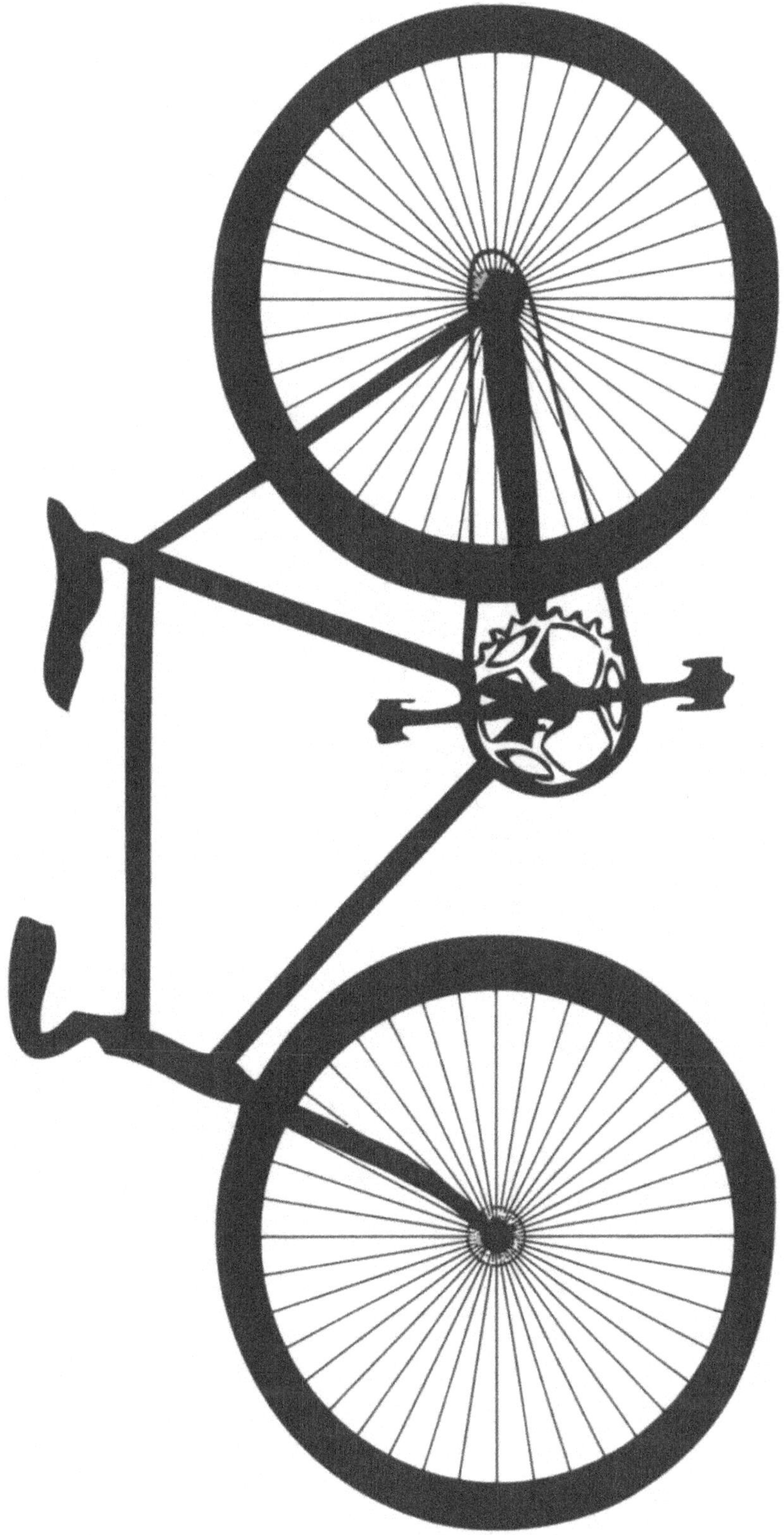

BICYCLE COLORING BOOK

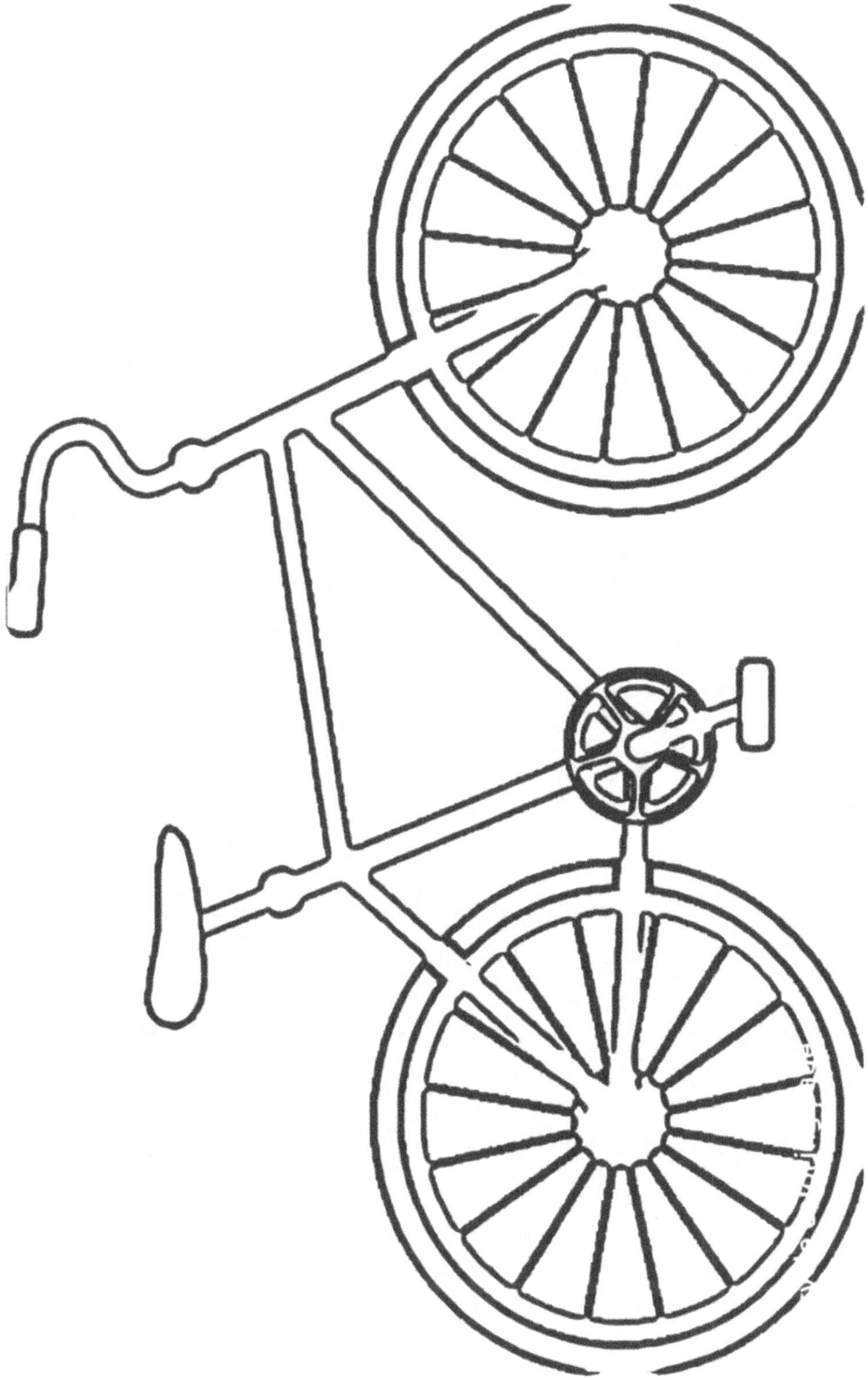

BICYCLE COLORING BOOK

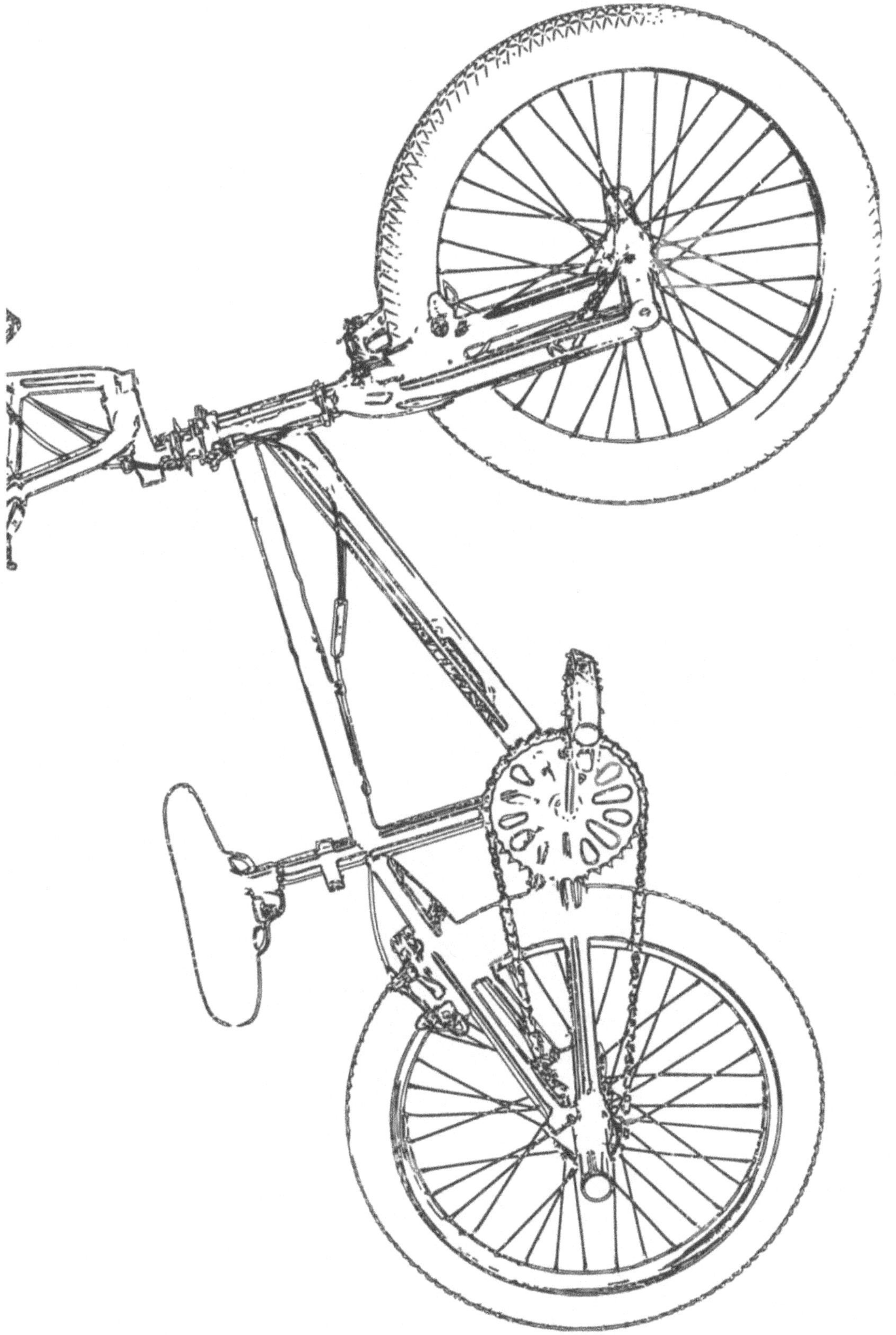

BICYCLE COLORING BOOK

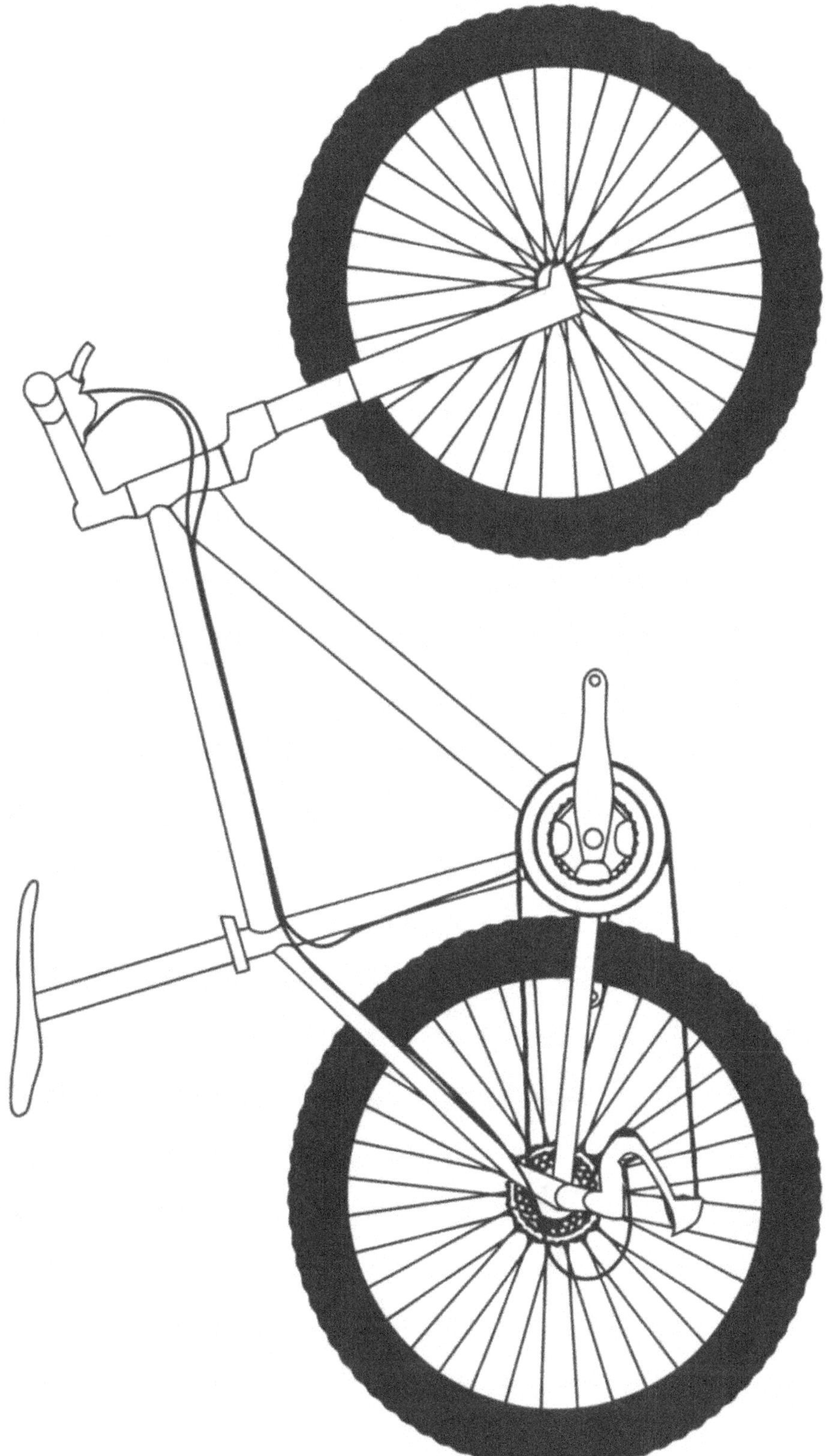

BICYCLE COLORING BOOK

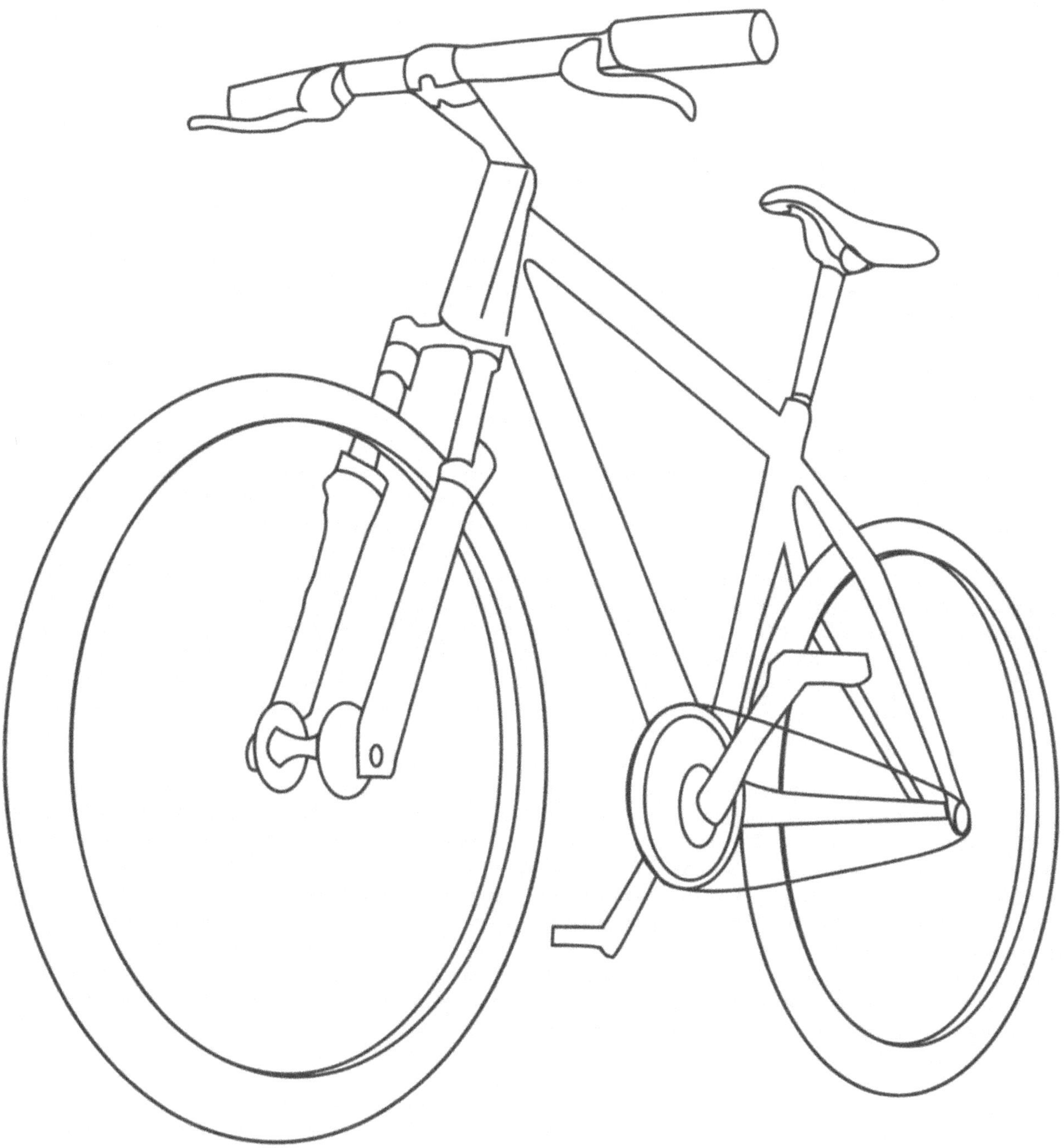

BICYCLE COLORING BOOK

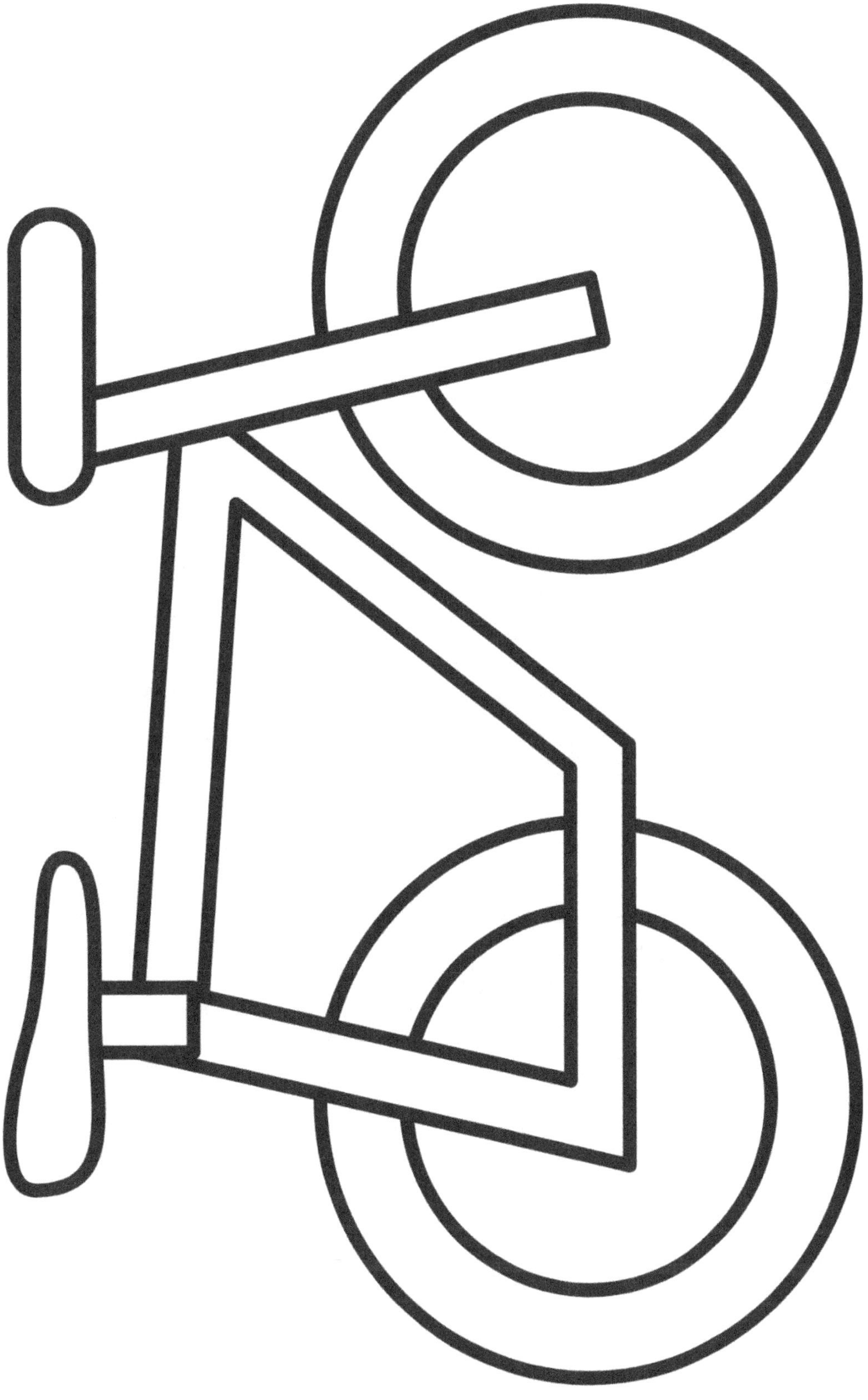

BICYCLE COLORING BOOK

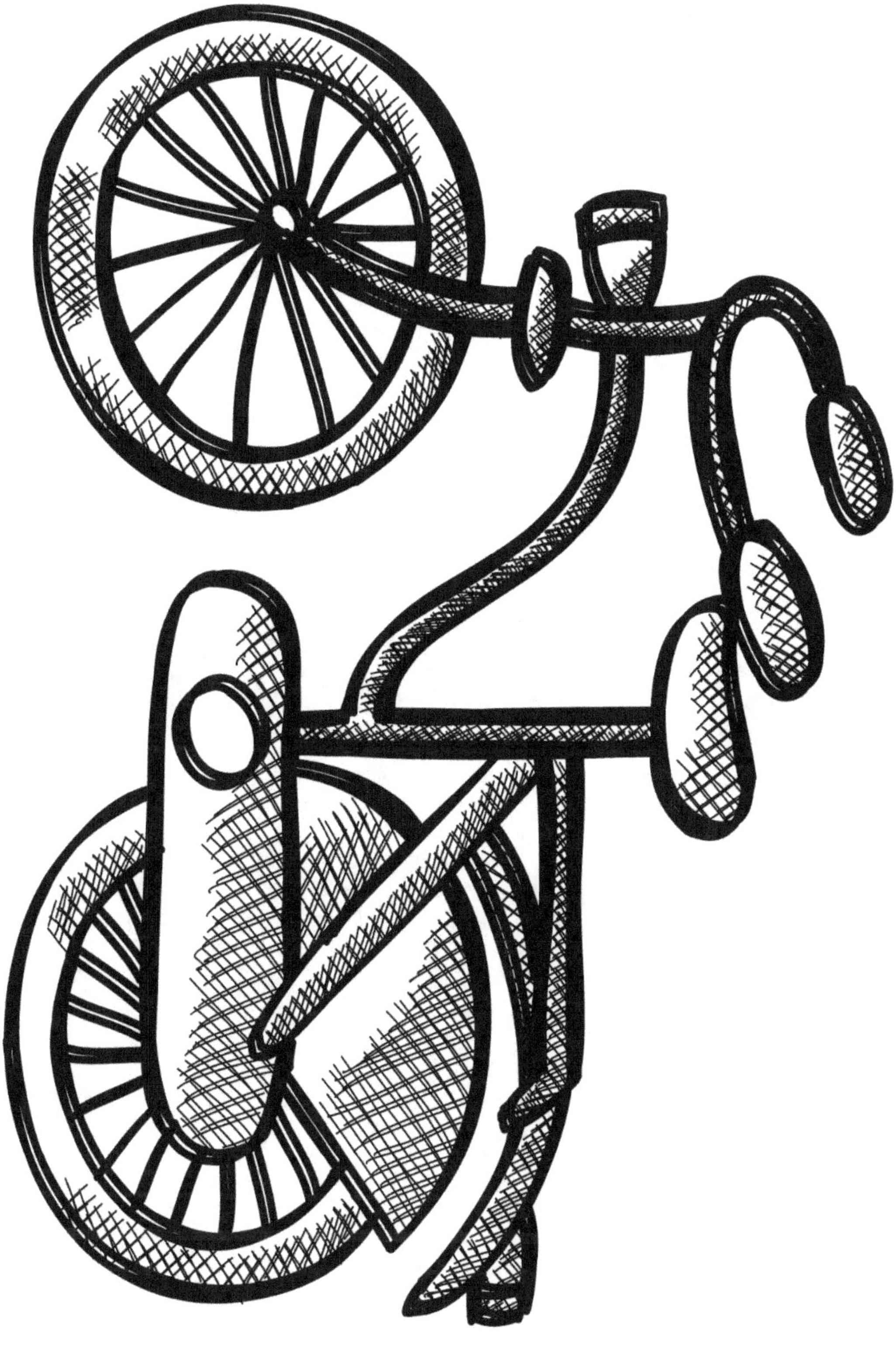

BICYCLE COLORING BOOK

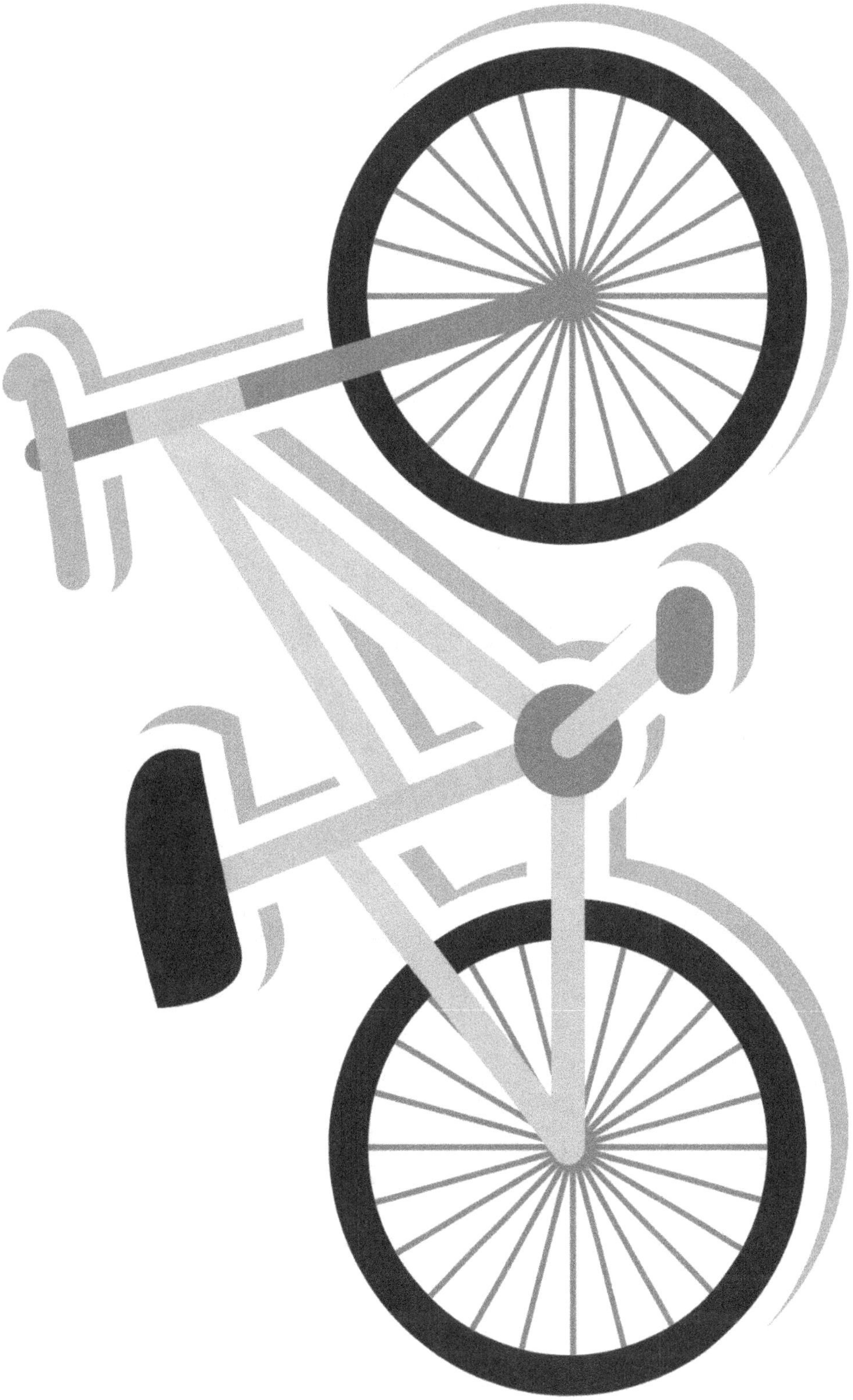

BICYCLE COLORING BOOK

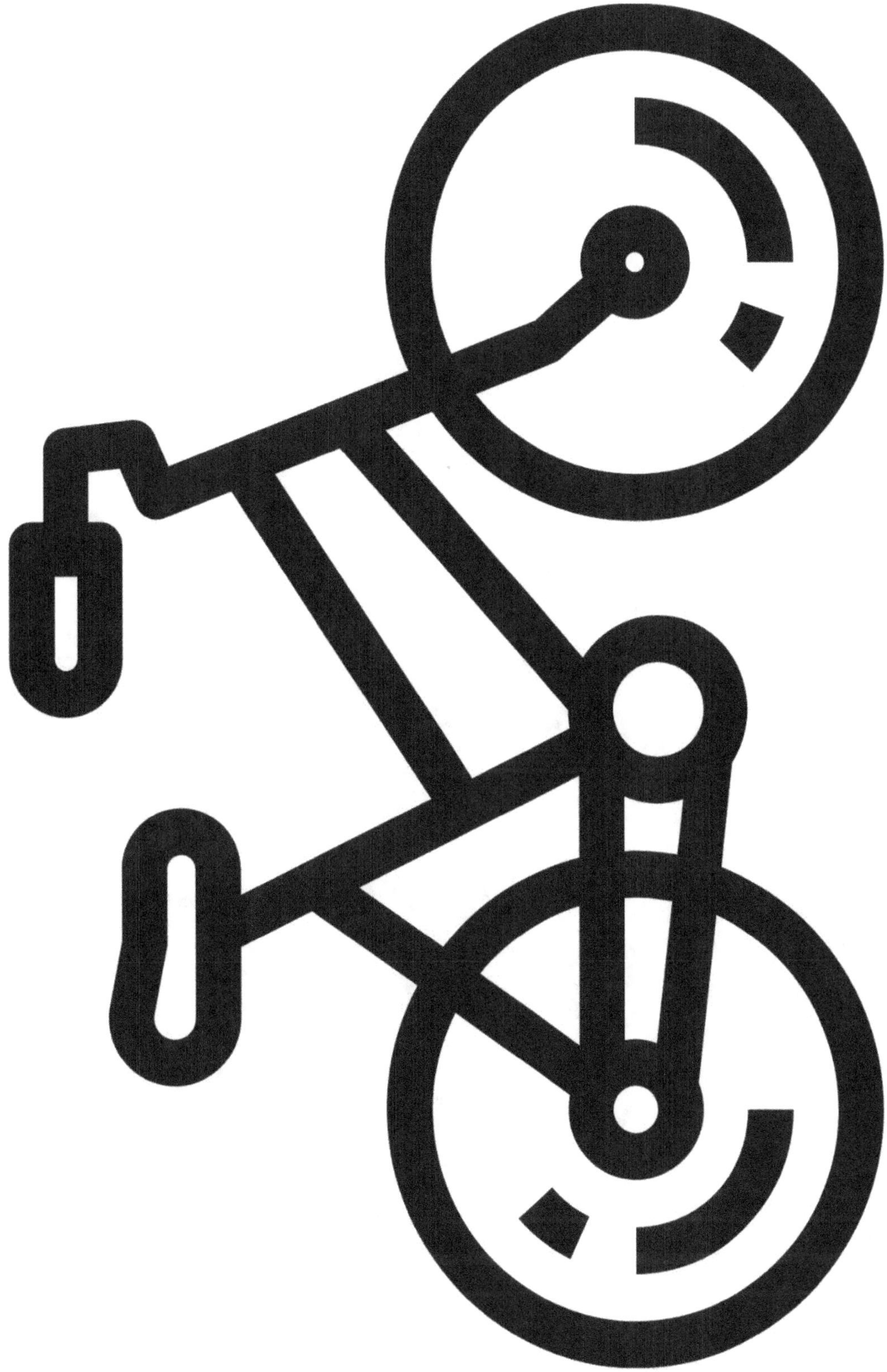

www.ingramcontent.com/pod-product-compliance
Lightning Source LLC
Chambersburg PA
CBHW060004230526
45472CB00008B/1944
* 9 7 9 8 6 8 1 3 9 0 1 2 1 *